Inspired Citizens

D1447087

JENNIE SWEET-CUSHMAN

Inspired Citizens

How Our Political Role Models
Shape American Politics

TEMPLE UNIVERSITY PRESS
Philadelphia • Rome • Tokyo

TEMPLE UNIVERSITY PRESS
Philadelphia, Pennsylvania 19122
tupress.temple.edu

Library of Congress Cataloging-in-Publication Data

Names: Sweet-Cushman, Jennie, 1976– author.
Title: Inspired citizens : how our political role models shape American
  politics / Jennie Sweet-Cushman.
Description: Philadelphia : Temple University Press, 2024. | Includes
  bibliographical references and index. | Summary: "Inspired Citizens
  enhances our understanding of how political role models function and
  affect political behavior in the United States. It explores what impact
  role models have on political participation and on candidate emergence,
  building a political science theory of role model effects which the
  author terms Inspired Citizenship Theory"— Provided by publisher.
Identifiers: LCCN 2023020545 (print) | LCCN 2023020546 (ebook) | ISBN
  9781439923481 (cloth) | ISBN 9781439923498 (paperback) | ISBN
  9781439923504 (pdf)
Subjects: LCSH: Political psychology—United States. | Role models—United
  States. | Political participation—United States. | Political
  candidates—United States.
Classification: LCC JA74.5 .S946 2024 (print) | LCC JA74.5 (ebook) | DDC
  320.01/9—dc23/eng/20230729
LC record available at https://lccn.loc.gov/2023020545
LC ebook record available at https://lccn.loc.gov/2023020546

For Leo:
Mamó loves you.

Contents

Acknowledgments

As everyone knows, the best part of any academic book is the acknowledgments. I am not sure if that says more about how exciting academic book acknowledgments are or how not exciting academic writing is, but regardless, I will try not to disappoint as I slather gratitude all over some folks who are more than deserving of it.

First, American politics is a tough thing to study these days. But as downtrodden as I may be by gridlock, intense partisan polarization, lack of participation, increasing political violence, and the erosion of civil and women's rights, the last few years have been helpful to my understanding of why I am a political scientist. I always kind of resonated with the idea that my motivation was as a critic of my native land, but increasingly I think it is because I am a patriot. And I like the idea of contributing, in some small way, to America fulfilling her potential. Role models feel like they have the potential to tap into the best of America, so this project has offered hope that was sorely needed.

I am indebted to Nancy Bocskor, the most well-connected woman/human I know, for helping me access data that would have otherwise been out of reach for me. I am also indebted to Nathan Kalmoe and Lilly Mason for sharing their measures on political aggression and political violence with me in advance of their own work coming out.

I appreciate my undergraduate students at Chatham University for listening—with interest—to me blather on about role models in my classes.

I also must recognize alums Trevor Gamble-Borsh ('21) for some assistance in compiling literature, Miranda Bruno ('21) for coding assistance, and especially the eternally devoted and brilliant Ava Roberts ('22), who served as a summer research assistant on this project. I am a lucky woman to get to teach and learn from such bright students year in and year out. I truly consider it the great privilege of my life to teach young people about American politics at Chatham University. Chatham also provides truly top-notch colleagues in the form of my "work wife" Carrie Tippen, Jessie Ramey, and Lou Martin, but also Katie Cruger, Karol Dean, and Lynne Bruckner, who have moved on to greener pastures.

Professionally, this gal could not have asked to have stumbled into a more supportive network of scholars. From day one, the political scientists (and occasional psychologists) in the subfield of gender and political psychology were not just producing good scholarship. They are forging a kinder, gentler place where work on gender and identity is taken seriously and valued. They are my people, my academic home, and the best bunch of scholars imaginable. I so appreciate all the guidance, support, and friendship I have received from them since I began my career. And while I am really grateful for the entire group, I must acknowledge both Nichole Bauer and Kathy Dolan, who provided encouragement and gave me valuable feedback on early drafts of this book. I need to thank supportive friends Mirya Holman, Melody Crowder-Meyer, Rosalynn Cooperman, Angie Bos, Monica Schneider, Rebecca Kreitzer, and especially my "virtual office mate," Erin Cassese, for all the assistance and fellowship they have shared. I am so fortunate.

In my personal life, there are just no words to aptly describe how big I hit in the life-partner lottery. Ray Cushman mostly has no idea what I do for a living, but that it is important to me means it is of utmost importance to him. This world's most generous man has been my constant supporter for over two decades, and my professional success, this book, and just about everything else I have ever set my mind to would be impossible without his support. I love this man more every single day, and that and the beautiful family we have made together are the things I am most grateful for in life. Shout out to that beautiful family, too. Love to my (mostly) tolerant kids: Brody, Kaden, Autumn, and Chris, along with wife Gina and baby Leo. Fur baby kitties Rebel and Justice mostly tried to sit on the keyboard and prevent book progress, but they also were great companions. Their feline brother, WHEELZ, is much too cool to be bothered with me, but he is a good boy nonetheless.

Finally, since I am about to do a lot of talking about role models in the pages that follow, I also want to note that I have had the best of all possible.

Gary Johnson nurtured me through a bachelor's degree in political science a million years ago and remains a source of constant support (and promises of lobster dinners when I reach milestones). May I never stop aspiring to be as thoughtful a teacher, as wise a researcher, as accomplished a writer, and as kind a mentor. He is—to quote Jane Austen viciously out of context—"the wisest and best of men." We should all be as lucky.

Inspired Citizens

1

Role Models in American Politics

In early 2017, every single one of my elected representatives in southwestern Pennsylvania, where I live and vote—from the president to my state representative to the mayor—was an older white man. For a scholar of gender and politics who focuses on political ambition and the value of diverse representation in politics, it was disheartening. In general, when women run for office, I get excited; when women run to represent me, I get really excited.

Imagine, then, my enthusiasm when a brilliant and poised young woman announced she would run that spring in a special election for a city council seat being vacated by one of these men. I had not even met her at this point. But this woman embodied everything I valued in a public servant, so I donated, I knocked on doors, I made phone calls, I worked the polls on election day, I even hosted a campaign event in my home. I was so inspired by this woman, this *role model*, that I sprung into political action. I wanted to participate deeply because I believed deeply in the profoundly impressive Erika Strassburger. Councilperson Strassburger is my role model.

I am not alone in my response to an inspirational figure. As Americans, we appear remarkably enamored with the idea that soccer player Megan Rapinoe might inspire young girls to want to play soccer or that Chadwick Boseman as the Black Panther would encourage little Black boys to feel powerful. People inspire others to do and feel great things in a host of realms—athletics, science, education, the arts. This narrative of role models provoking others to consider new ideas plays extremely well into the idea of American exceptionalism; exceptional Americans inspire other Americans to be exceptional, too. This book focuses on the impact role models have in the realm of politics through the lens of political psychology.

Social scientists have evaluated the impact of role models for decades. Research on social learning theory (Bandura 1969, 1986; Smith and Hitt 2005) in psychology points to numerous domains where the presence of role models can effectively model aspirational behavior, represent the possible, and provide inspiration (Morgenroth, Ryan, and Peters 2015). Recent scholarship has looked at everything from how role models motivate good surgeons (Stephens and Dearani 2021) to how they encourage physical activity (Hayes 2022) or provoke a greater interest in entrepreneurship (Abbasianchavari and Moritz 2021).

Additionally, role models with whom we share defining characteristics, or "ingroup" role models, also have the potential to motivate where stereotypes might otherwise suppress achievement (Dasgupta 2011). A role model—someone whose "behaviours, styles and attributes are emulated by others" (Singh, Vinnicombe, and James 2006, 1)—can affect the academic performance of groups who might typically struggle, inspire nontraditional career choices, and encourage persistence in the face of adversity (see Ahn, Hu, and Vega 2020 for a review in education research).

In some circumstances, however, the presence of certain types of role models might leave citizens feeling overwhelmed or unmotivated because they believe they do not possess similar essential qualities (Betz and Sekaquaptewa 2012; Cheryan, Drury, and Vichayapai 2013; Sweet-Cushman 2018a; Schneider, Sweet-Cushman, and Gordon 2023). Other times, we are all channeling the late Supreme Court justice Ruth Bader Ginsburg ready to graduate at the top of our class and carve out a legal legacy despite the barriers we face (Bader Ginsburg 2016). This leaves us without a unified theory of how citizens—and especially marginalized ones—may be impacted by the presence of role models. But, as I reveal, this complexity affords much potential for understanding how individualized role models might be best utilized to increase political participation and strengthen American democracy. As Gibson (2004, 134) notes, role models provide "cognitive constructions *based on an individual's needs, wants, and ambitions*" (emphasis mine) to guide individual development.

Role Models in American Politics?

Politics is also a realm where many individuals may face barriers to their development as civically engaged citizens. However, we have limited evidence of a role model phenomenon at play in the political realm. Particularly for those who belong to groups that have been historically marginalized, does seeing people like themselves involved in politics encourage them to do the same? While research in psychology applies role modeling theories in an abundance of contexts, political science focuses on those who have been marginalized—largely girls and women—in exploring these effects. This scholarship can be largely divided into two categories of contribution: role model effects on general political participation and role model effects on candidate emergence.

Despite these contributions, empirical research in political science fails to comprehensively examine role model effects in three ways. First, researchers have generated an abundance of research on how gender impacts political participation but have done little to consider the intersectionality that surrounds these questions. The seminal contributions in this area focus largely on adolescent girls (Campbell and Wolbrecht 2006, 2020; Wolbrecht and Campbell 2007) and point to a largely positive impact of the presence of high-profile women in politics, though Mariani, Marshall, and Mathews-Schultz (2015) found that these effects are mediated in different ways by ideology and party. There might also be some evidence that it can be demotivating for young people and Black women (Shames 2015, 2017). However, we know very little about how adult political participation and attitudes in the United States are impacted by role models (but see Wolak 2015) when the psychological literature would suggest that role models have the potential to affect everyone.

One element of adult participation that has been examined in recent years for evidence of a role model effect is candidate emergence—the likelihood of individuals putting themselves forward as candidates for political office. Again primarily focusing only on the impact on women, studies from different scholars outside the United States point alternatively to the presence of women in politics (e.g., potential role models) having a temporarily positive effect on the number of women running for office (Gilardi 2015 in Switzerland) or to a largely positive longer-term effect (Beaman et al. 2009, 2012; Bhavnani 2009; Deininger and Liu 2013). U.S.-based research has been less conclusive on this front, with research ranging from providing evidence of a null effect (Broockman 2014) to evidence of a substantially positive one (Ladam, Harden, and Windett 2018). Pulling primarily from observational data, these analyses limit evidence of a role model effect to descriptive representation—the presence of women on the ballot or in elective office.

Experimental work, too, presents disparate results. Brief exposure in an experimental treatment from an unknown role model seems to yield no impact in several applications (Foos and Gilardi 2020; Holman and Schneider 2018), while a more sustained role model exposure did provoke greater ambition for those who identified most strongly with the role model (Sweet-Cushman 2018a). These conflictual findings present the second gap in the literature this book will fill.

And finally, there is no comprehensive or systematic effort to theory build along these lines in political science. There is no clear picture about the effect of role models in American politics, despite the conventional wisdom that role models are universally inspirational. Multiple other fields have drawn on social psychology to provide insight into role model effects—a decades-old and mature field of research. Research in psychology provides insight into the complexity we have yet to fully examine in political science since psychology often reveals that role models have multifaceted effects that lead to a host of outcomes. Role models may signal what is expected of us through socialization mechanisms, as social learning theory would suggest (Bandura 1986; Eagly 2013). Without an understanding of these signals, we are left without a nuanced and unified theory of how citizens—and especially marginalized ones—may be impacted by the presence of role models. But, as I reveal in this book, this complexity affords much potential for understanding how role models might be best utilized to increase political participation and strengthen American democracy. Thus, I identify *when* we are likely to see role model effects occur and *how* these effects work.

Inspired Citizens?

I ground these findings in a psychological theory, built from social role theory in psychology, that I call Inspired Citizenship Theory (see Figure 1.1). Inspired Citizenship Theory considers the often-conflicting pressures and messages political role models project to citizens and posits that role models inspire political action most effectively when they fulfill highly individualized expectations for role model identity, spurring deeper connection and a desire to emulate. These expectations include patterns well established in the psychological literature, like role model attainability, identification, and traits. It integrates the explanatory power of two complementary theories that frequently do not engage with one another in psychology: the Motivational Theory of Role Modeling (Morgenroth, Ryan, and Peters 2015) and the Stereotype Inoculation Model (Dasgupta 2011).

Inspired Citizenship Theory (ICT) injects into the study of American politics the idea that political role models have the potential to strengthen American democracy. Identification with a personal political role mod-

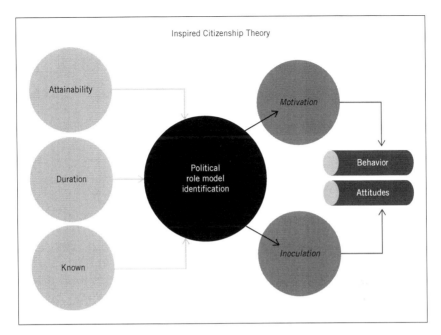

Figure 1.1 Theoretical Framework of Inspired Citizenship Theory

el is at the theory's core. That is, for role model effects in politics to be detectible, an individual has to have made a connection with someone who provokes them to think differently about and engage with politics. Importantly, this is not the same as descriptive representation, which is making individual citizens' voices "present" in politics by virtue of those doing the representing merely resembling those being represented (Pitkin 1967). Most of the research in political science and political psychology could more aptly be described as studying the effect of descriptive representation (i.e., the presence of some group) when referring to role model effects.

Arguably, in many ways feeling a personal connection to someone who can be identified as a political role model should be more potent than descriptive representation—which does not guarantee a personal relationship and, in fact, more often than not probably entirely lacks one. Personal relationships are essential to both motivational and inoculation mechanisms of role models and thus to role model effects. Furthermore, descriptive representation either exists or does not at the macro level, whether or not a citizen acknowledges it. Identifying with a political role model happens at the individual level and, by definition, can be acknowledged by the individual identifying (the aspirant). This distinction is important for my purposes—and the purposes of ICT—because I, as the researcher, am guaranteed of a relationship for those who have a political role model. Descriptive representation does not necessarily offer this same guarantee.

Of course, it is not likely that everyone has a political role model, but for those who do, ICT suggests that there are two primary potential functions of that role model. First, in keeping with the Motivational Theory of Role Modeling (MTRM), role models have the power to motivate behavior, affect, or attitudes. This may take many forms. I focus on just a handful of important political behaviors and attitudes in this book, broadly arguing that role model effects may bolster engagement in politics and positive political attitudes like political trust. Similarly, these relationships have the potential to dampen normatively negative attitudes like support for political violence. Second, in keeping with the Stereotype Inoculation Model (SIM), these same political behaviors or attitudes might be further impacted when an aspirant identifies with a role model with whom they share an identity.

ICT also posits that the context of the relationship with a role model can moderate the effectiveness of these influences. Interwoven in the MTRM literature is the preeminent importance of three factors that are relevant to political role models. Role model effects may hinge on how attainable a role model is (Lockwood and Kunda 1997), with unattainable role models suppressing aspirational behavior. The duration of the role model relationship is also important, with longer-term relationships offering the accumulation of inspiration (Turban, Dougherty, and Lee 2002). A final factor is the type of exposure an aspirant or potential aspirant has to a role model (Shin, Levy, and London 2016). The type of exposure depends on what aspect of social life a role model relationship is being examined, but in politics I interpret this to be how well known a role model is to the aspirant. These three features of the aspirant–role model relationship have the power to "switch on" a more pronounced role model effect.

Using ICT as a backdrop, this book explores who Americans identify with as role models and the implications for their political participation in both the general citizenry (i.e., mass population) and the elite citizenry (e.g., candidates for public office). In doing so, I draw on original datasets, unique measures, and novel experiments to facilitate the individual-level and subject-driven analyses that have been frequently absent in political science role model research. This approach allows me to make a significant theoretical contribution that expands our understanding of how complex socialization is crucial to democratic engagement.

Put most simply, I extend work in social psychology by offering a new theory of role model effects on the entire realm of American political participation. While still limited, extant research on role models in the U.S.

context reveals that they have the potential to impact citizen participation in a multitude of ways. In the big picture, productively used role models have the potential to encourage greater, deeper, and more diverse citizen political participation, as a more committed and engaged citizenry is a hallmark of healthy democracy. At the individual level, it explains why Councilperson Strassburger provoked me to get off my couch and do so much more to engage in my political environment and ultimately feel much more positively about it. I am keenly interested in ways we might harness this to encourage others as well.

Outline of *Inspired Citizens*

This book examines the complex interaction between political role models and their aspirants through three primary research questions. First, *who are our political role models?* This research reveals whether the contemporary political environment genuinely and to what magnitude includes people who inspire our political behavior and attitudes. It identifies who these individuals are, what traits they possess, and the mechanisms by which citizens believe they are being encouraged (or discouraged) to engagement by the presence of these exemplary individuals.

Second, *how do role models impact who participates in politics in America and how they do it?* Having established a connection with political role models, I can then illuminate how Americans identify with their political role models. I establish how identification with role models varies, particularly among those who have been historically marginalized in American politics. At the heart of this examination is how role models may or may not inspire everyday citizens to be politically engaged. I argue the compelling need to inspire faith and trust in the political system by holding others up as examples of what is possible if citizens engage. Maybe more Americans need political role models, or maybe they need options for different ones.

Along these same lines, I also consider these effects on political candidates by asking the question, *how do role models impact who runs for political office and why?* The most profound commitment to American politics is often attributed to candidates for political office, which is the rarest form of political participation and the least representative (Verba, Schlozman, and Brady 1995). I thus expand my analysis of the effect of role models to consider those who take the ultimate plunge into representative democracy and run for office. Here, I again focus on how these role model effects might be most crucial to those who see themselves represented in American politics less frequently.

I begin Chapter 2 with an outline of the breadth of psychological research on role models in the vein of both MTRM and SIM. I organize the streams that speak specifically to political role models. Since these existing theories have yet to be used—let alone integrated—to explain political behavior or attitudes, I build on these foundations to present the Inspired Citizenship Theory of political role model effects.

In Chapter 3, I provide a background of the understanding we have of descriptive representation and role model effects in political science, carefully defining the differences and relationship between these two concepts. I outline what we know about how both mass and elite populations appear to respond to role models and reveal the gaps in our understanding. I then outline what ICT can help us further understand about both mass and elite political engagement.

With ICT as a guide, I examine the effect of role models in mass (everyday citizen) and elite (political candidate) samples by exploring two primary predictions. The first, the *Inspired Citizenship Motivation Prediction*, anticipates that connections with political role models will be associated with different political behavior and political attitudes than those of Americans without these relationships. The second, the *Inspired Citizenship Inoculation Prediction*, expects that having a political role model who shares your identity will have additional power in enhancing political engagement, especially for some groups of Americans.

I investigate these predictions in both mass public (general population) and elite public (political candidates) samples. Chapter 4 draws upon a large and reasonably representative survey of U.S. citizens ($n = 1,723$) using the Lucid Theorem platform to solicit responses to close-ended and open-ended survey questions. Analysis of this data allows me to paint a full picture of whom citizens identify as role models and what traits they embody, as well as to make connections between role model traits and increased political participation.

In Chapter 5, I apply ICT to those making arguably the most significant participatory commitment to American politics: running for elective office. This chapter draws upon a large survey of individuals running for state-level and congressional offices during the 2020 election cycle. This sampling frame represents one (though not the only) population likely to have been influenced to run for political office by someone they had seen also participate in electoral politics. Identifying the role models who have inspired these individuals will shed light on inspired citizens in action. I again explore the exposure and traits these role models possess but add to the analysis an examination of the connection between the role model and the candidate, focusing on historically underrepresented intersections of racial and gender identities. This methodological approach helps make connections between political role models and political elites, revealing important facets of ICT. Isolating the impact of political role models allows for theory building and contextualization and sets up further research into causal mechanisms in the relationship between political role models and the political participation and attitudes of the general population.

Since survey data does not allow me to distinguish between what is a role model effect and what is simply people with role models being systematically different from those without, I also isolate the effect of role models experimentally. I again examine both a mass public and an elite public sample. In Chapter 6, I again draw on a Lucid sample of American citizens ($n = 631$) who are prompted to select a (personal) role model. These participants are then exposed to political messages from their chosen role model, and I measure how that exposure impacts their intent to participate in politics and political attitudes as compared to those who receive the same messages without attribution to their role model. This methodology allows me to isolate only the role model effects.

I use a field experiment to look for role model effects in an elite sample of women ($n = 66$) in Chapter 7. In this quasi-experiment, I treat a campaign training as a role model intervention. Participants in the training are asked to identify one of the training's speakers who resonated with them as a role model. I then examine, before and after training, how that role model exposure impacted the potential for candidate emergence. This very applied approach to the use of role models identifies not only role model effects but also a way they may be used to inspire and inoculate a group historically marginalized in politics (women).

In conclusion, I consider the normative implications of this research in Chapter 8. If political participation, as Verba and Nie (1972) famously argue, "is at the heart of democratic theory and at the heart of the democratic political formula in the United States" (3), then understanding how political role models may inspire or depress participation in the general public and affect who runs for office may be essential. Who should we identify with as a political role model to best serve representative democracy? What does that relationship need to look like to be effective? The answers revealed in this book will help strengthen our understanding of what we should and should not look to political figures for in guiding democratic behaviors and inspiring productive citizenship.

2

The Psychological Impact of Role Models

Imitation is the sincerest form of flattery that mediocrity
can pay to greatness.

—OSCAR WILDE

To appreciate what role models do, first consider how we learn how
to do or be anything throughout the course of our lives. Whether it
is learning to tie our shoes, manage our to-do lists, or function in
interpersonal relationships, we form our own skills through both conscious
and unconscious learning from those around us. This socialization has
wide-ranging impacts on our lives from small things, like how we fold our
laundry, to the most significant life choices, like what careers we choose
for ourselves—and everything in between.

This process of becoming who we are as individuals is ultimately a product of socialization. Individuals' social environment interacts with their
biological predispositions to form their unique systems of behavior (Child
1954). Socialization is a foundational concept in psychology and forms the
basis of much of our understanding of human behavior, especially in how
it relates to the unique features of each individual's environment. Agents
of socialization are highly individualized but generally start with: educational influences, media consumption, religious influences, and friends and
extended family. These influences combine to mold individuals into who
they are and how they behave in the world. Role models are an essential
component of this process.

Social Cognitive Theory Perspective

Socialization is the mechanism behind role modeling. Whether explicitly or implicitly, successful role models demonstrate the norms and expected behavior of an organizational sphere and communicate social knowledge and effective behaviors in the context in which they are perceived. Those who emulate the modeler are more likely to behave in ways that are also effective in that context. Those who are subconsciously influenced by role models are intuitively better prepared to exist in the environment they have absorbed information about. Those who seek out role models may consciously recognize behaviors that are beneficial to emulate. While this book focuses on role models selected by individuals, it is important to note that someone can be a role model and embody all those attributes without the role model or their target recognizing it. This latter scenario more aptly applies in politics to the impact of descriptive representation, which I discuss more fully in Chapter 3.

One vein of socialization research focuses on social learning. Much of the research that exists on this process examines experiential learning. I bet most readers will appreciate how this learning is exemplified by their ability to tie their shoes. Like most adults, I still tie my shoes using the "bunny ears method" because that is how I watched my mom demonstrate it over and over again when I was three and four years old. I learned this skill through social learning, with my mom serving as my shoe-tying role model. It is an exceptionally common form of learning how to do something for oneself. In fact, the connection between learning and doing is so strong that as the anthropologist Gladys Reichard (1938) once noted, in many languages there are not even separate words for "teach" and "show."

Social learning relies on four cognitive processes: attention, retention, motor reproduction, and motivation and reinforcement. Each of these present an opportunity for modeled behavior to influence the behavior of others, and thus we see the powerful potential of role models. Indeed, as the pioneer of psychological modeling, Albert Bandura (1986, 47), argues, modeling behavior is "one of the most powerful means of transmitting values, attitudes, and patterns of thought and behaviour." Aspirants note the behavior of another and internalize the patterns that were followed. They are then motivated to replicate the behavior by the perception that there is sufficient positive reward for doing so, and they then engage in the same or similar act themselves. An oversimplification, for sure, but one that feels intuitively applicable to how we use role models in our day-to-day lives.

Role models, then, socialize others primarily by way of their actions. As Bandura (2021) wrote in his seminal work on social learning, "modeling influences operate principally through their informative function, and that observers acquire mainly symbolic representations of modeled events rather than specific stimulus-response associations" (16). We are unlikely to attempt something new if we think we will be unsuccessful at it (Bandura 1997; Wigfield and Eccles 2000). So, whether that is a new relationship, a new hobby, a new profession, or even tying your shoes, seeing someone else accomplish the thing we would like to attempt is a potentially powerful motivator.

Role Model Effects

The power of role models has been explored in myriad contexts. Scholars have dug deeply into how role models might be useful in making STEM fields more diverse (Betz and Sekaquaptewa 2012; Cheryan et al. 2011), how they encourage success in college (Ahn, Hu, and Vega 2020; Bettinger and Long 2005), and how students choose their field of study (Nauta and Kokaly 2001). Others have focused on how role modeling impacts leadership (Hoyt, Burnette, and Innella 2012; Hoyt and Simon 2011). In the following, I discuss how many of these studies enrich our understanding of the potential that lies in the social learning that comes with role models.

Scholars have long noted the fragmentation that exists in role models research (Irvine 1989), and this remains largely true. Nonetheless, this large volume of research can predominantly be tied to two complementary theories in social psychology, MTRM (Morgenroth, Ryan, and Peters 2015) and SIM (Dasgupta 2011). These theories align with different aspects of social learning theory, which make them intuitively complementary.

Motivational Theory of Role Modeling

The first, the Motivational Theory of Role Modeling (Morgenroth, Ryan, and Peters 2015), is primarily built around "motivation and reinforcement" as the cognitive process that Bandura identified in social learning. MTRM centers the aspirant in that it considers both the relevant attributes of the aspirant and those of the role model themselves. This theory is the more general theory of the two and is applicable in analyzing just about any scenario where role model influence might be a consideration. MTRM considers the impact of role models on an aspirant's motivation and both existing and potential goals by focusing on aspirant perception of three role model traits: goal embodiment, attainability, and desirability (Morgenroth, Ryan, and Peters 2015).

This framework argues that role models serve three primary functions. They provide a model of behavior, represent what may be achievable, and inspire role aspirants in their own endeavors (Morgenroth, Ryan, and Peters 2015). This orientation is consistent with Bandura's (1969, 1986, 2021) motivational process in that the positive outcomes revealed by the role model are likely to reinforce the possibility of imitation.

Scholars of mentoring networks have noted that role models come from two dimensions: whether they are close or distant to the aspirant and whether an aspirant's role model network includes those from few or many domains (Higgins and Kram 2001; Singh, Vinnicombe, and James 2006). The domains include family, friends, business, arts, fictitious, royal, political, "female," and "male." Parents, for example, serve as potent role models for their children's future careers (Basow and Howe 1980). A powerful example of this influence is seen in military families, where both sons and daughters are more likely to pursue a military career if they have had a parent or parents who served (Smith and Rosenstein 2017). But as adulthood approaches, new influences begin to take precedence. Professionally, role models may come from entrepreneurial or career influences and may be most useful when they have experienced similar barriers (Singh, Vinnicombe, and James 2006).

As individuals move through life, they collect role models from other domains. These role models must have been clearly successful and competent (Marx et al. 2013; Marx and Ko 2012) in an individual's area of interest, though they do not need to have had direct contact (Marx and Roman 2002) or be personally known to the aspirant. Some scholars have drawn on Higgins's (1987) theory of "self," which divides an individual's self-concept into three conceptions: the actual self, the ideal self, and the "ought" self, the latter of which includes traits an individual feels somehow obligated to embody. If behavioral change is associated with role model behavior (Bandura 2001; Krueger and Brazeal 1994; Sosik and Godshalk 2000), then evaluating which of these self-concepts is most at play in this change could be critical to effective use of role models. Radu and Loué (2008), in a small study of business students, found that a realistic "ideal self" framing was more effective than a more negative "ought self" framing—especially for those who were relatively less invested in the possibility of behavior change. The negative effect of ought-self framing appears to be mediated by goal congruence; those aspiring to success or promotion are buoyed by positive depictions of role models, while those more concerned about avoiding the consequences of a behavior change are more likely to respond to a negatively presented role model (Lockwood, Jordan, and Kunda 2002).

Role model effects have been extensively studied in the realm of women in education and career choice. Role models in this context are important because they embody educational or career goals and illustrate a path to achieving them (Collins 1996; Lockwood and Kunda 1997). The overarching finding in this body of literature is that role model impact varies based on a host of factors attributed to the relational context with the role model but that the relationship is mediated by self-efficacy.

The preponderance of scholarship examining role models in academic settings is focused on the possibility that role models could be helpful in addressing inequities in STEM education. Recognizing that the United States likely will need more doctors, computer scientists, and engineers in the coming years, addressing women's resiliency in STEM disciplines is crucial (Carnevale, Smith, and Melton 2011; Carnevale, Smith, and Strohl 2010). Other underrepresented groups have received relatively little attention in the literature (but see Elliott et al. 1996). STEM courses tend to have lower success rates than their non-STEM equivalents, and STEM majors have a higher dropout rate than other courses of study (Holden and Lander 2012; Strenta et al. 1994).

This positive modeling impact appears not to be specific to STEM. A large-N study (54,000 observations) published in 2005 (but using 1998 and 1999 enrollment data) joins others that reveal that the gender of instructors matters to disciplinary patterns of major and course selection. For female students in fields where they are underrepresented (e.g., geology, mathematics, statistics), female faculty had the potential to—though did not universally—encourage female college students to continue to explore or major in their field. The authors found similar effects for men in fields where men are underrepresented (e.g., education and social work) (Bettinger and Long 2005).

Most of this research assesses how role models motivate undergraduates to make major and/or career selections or persist in their chosen field. However, women graduate students pursuing Ph.Ds. are also more likely to succeed if they have women mentors (Neumark and Gardecki 1996), though women tend to be underrepresented in these roles as well. In another instance, cadets at the U.S. Naval Academy appeared to feel more positive about their abilities and more favorably about their career as naval officers because of the intentional mentoring of more senior students. Male students responded more positively to male peers while the gender did not matter for women, who responded equally positively to male and female role models (Smith and Rosenstein 2017).

When women as role models in academia and elsewhere are found to be demotivating for female students, it is likely due to stereotype violation (Betz and Sekaquaptewa 2012). Aspirants hold ideas about who is and who is not appropriate or qualified for certain social roles. If they themselves do not match the characteristics or traits held by the appropriate type of person, they are apt to be deterred to move themselves in the direction of modeling. This phenomenon, stereotype threat, is where the second predominant role model theory comes in.

Stereotype Inoculation Model

The second theory, the Stereotype Inoculation Model (Dasgupta 2011), is more focused on understanding perhaps the most common way role model research has been applied: as a highly utilitarian means of combating underrepresentation in professional, organizational, and educational environments. This model tends more to the other three of Bandura's processes—attention, retention, and motor reproduction—as it focuses significantly on the "do as I say / do as I do" aspects of role modeling. The SIM framework considers important context-based factors that make role models more or less effective in encouraging those who have been otherwise marginalized.

SIM focuses on how role models serve to alleviate the negative impact of underrepresentation in a context and "inoculate" an aspirant from potential stereotype threats (Dasgupta 2011). This model is thus most concerned with how role models might be used in serving normative goals like increasing diversity in areas that have historically lacked it. This is where my interest in theories of role models lie and where ICT potentially has the most to contribute to the realm of politics.

Politics is similar to many of the arenas where SIM has been used to consider the impact role models may have. The assumption is that individuals who have been traditionally marginalized in a field that has been historically dominated by white, affluent, cisgender, heterosexual, and/or Christian men might have been socialized to stereotype certain societal roles as being consistent with these identities and not their own. Diekman et al. (2011) document this phenomenon in terms of certain careers as goals. These psychologists demonstrate that career selection is associated with an individual's career goals (communal or agentic) and that careers may be stereotypically considered more communal or more agentic. If an individual values communal goals but views a career as one that achieves agentic goals (or vice versa), that mismatch can demotivate someone from pursuing that career. Role models in those fields play an important role in communicating those stereotypes. When these individuals embody characteristics that do not match our own, we may be discouraged from following in their footsteps. Alternatively, when they are like us, it may pave the way for us to pursue the same path they have. Indeed, perceived similarity to a role model has been shown to mediate whether individuals anticipate that they will also be successful in that role model's field (Cheryan et al. 2011). In many cases this means the role model should be of the same gender or ethnic group (Lockwood 2006; Marx and Goff 2005; Marx and Roman 2002; McIntyre, Paulson, and Lord 2003).

However, in STEM, whether or not role models embody STEM stereotypes has been shown to be more important than whether they are an ingroup member (Cheryan et al. 2011). For example, researchers have examined whether exposure to a stereotypical role model in the field of computer science would negatively impact female undergraduates' interest in the field. They found that regardless of the role model's gender, even a brief exposure—merely two minutes in this study—to the stereotypical role model had a tangible and enduring negative impact on the interest of the study's female participants (Cheryan, Drury, and Vichayapai 2013).

Furthermore, a highly successful role model can actually suppress the positive impact the role model may have (Lockwood and Kunda 1997), but similarity with role models along identity lines can moderate stereotype threats that are provoked by the perception of unattainability in a dissimilar role model (Marx and Ko 2012). If role models are out of reach, there may be a "negative social comparison" that depresses achievement (Collins 1996). Priming someone with neutral or achievable information has a positive impact, but even one's own "highest hopes" lead to discouragement (Lockwood and Kunda 1999). Researchers have taken this to mean that effective role models will emphasize their struggles and the barriers they had to overcome to achieve their success.

An evaluation of a program designed to expose at-risk Mexican American women to presentations from successful role models illustrates this point well. This study found that a well-intentioned presentation may not be sufficient without presenting "the cumulative nature of success" (Hernandez 1995). In other words, success is rarely linear, and unrealistic presentations of role models who seemingly never dealt with adversity may discourage those they intend to inspire.

Inspired Citizenship Theory

For whatever reason, even though MTRM and SIM overlap significantly in social psychology, academic discussions of role models have mostly not permeated the silos in which each theory currently exists. However, given the way identity has always shaped American politics, both theories seem essential to understanding the importance of role models in this domain. Participation in politics in the United States is in no way compulsory, and thus something is required to motivate democratic behaviors and ideals—something role models seem both intuitively and empirically capable of, lending credence to MTRM. Role models also seem likely to offer a way to overcome barriers that many members of American society face in cultivating democratic engagement—which SIM has promise to provide insight into. As such, I integrate both into the formulation of ICT.

A healthy democracy arguably requires its citizenry to tap into all four of social learning's cognitive processes. Citizens must pay *attention* to democratic process, norms, and expectations. They need *retention* of important concepts, structures, and phenomenon. They will need to re-create the *motor reproduction* required to engage with institutions and other citizens. And, importantly, they will require the not insignificant *motivation and reinforcement* that are essential to engagement. ICT posits that a powerful way to cultivate these four cognitive processes in politics is via political role models who emulate them.

As MTRM (Morgenroth, Ryan, and Peters 2015) has demonstrated in a multitude of other areas, role models in politics hold the potential to model political behaviors, exhibit what is achievable as a result of political engagement, and inspire aspirants in their own political orientations. SIM (Dasgupta 2011) holds the additional promise that political role models can help counteract marginalizing forces in American politics that might prevent women; LGBTIA+ Americans; racial, ethnic, and religious minorities; or others from fully engaging as political citizens. This would be especially true if these role models shared an identity with the aspirant. Seeing someone who has faced the same barriers in political thought and action as you overcome those barriers offers a protective inoculation against marginalization in politics.

ICT thus first argues that Americans who identify with political role models will be different from those who do not. This means two complementary things. First, those who aspire to engage meaningfully in politics will be apt to seek out political role models to identify with. Second, it also means that those role models will set examples that can be followed by those they have connected with on some level.

While the impact of role models may hypothetically be conditioned by any number of things, three factors appear regularly in role model research and seem relevant to the political behavior and attitudes applicable to ICT. These factors, or what I call *role model orientation*, are the attainability of the role model's success, the duration of the connection with the role model, and how close the role model relationship is (i.e., how well known the role model is to the aspirant).

The attainability of a role model speaks to how realistic the role model's accomplishments are. As Lockwood and Kunda (2000) describe, how successful a role model is perceived to be may be the switch that determines whether the role model has a positive (encouraging the aspirational behavior or attitudes) or a negative (depressing the aspirational behavior or attitudes) impact on the aspirant. This makes intuitive sense in that if we admire someone, we are going to feel much more hopeful in emulating them if we actually believe we can. If their accomplishments are too great, it may just discourage us from making much of an effort to try. For example, one study found that in an experiment that required participants to complete a leadership task, exposure to a high-level role model depressed perceived performance and bolstered feelings of inferiority while increasing perceived task difficulty (Hoyt and Simon 2011). ICT anticipates that those who have political role models whose success feels out of reach, and especially those aspiring to electoral office, will be similarly impacted.

In developing this theory, I also recognize that some connections with role models are deeper than others, and how long the relationship has persisted and how close it is are essential considerations. The duration of the relationship with a role model is a consideration discussed at length in the literature on mentoring, which is arguably a type of intentional role modeling. Turban, Dougherty, and Lee (2002) found that the duration of the role model relationship moderated how similar someone felt to their mentor, which in turn can make a relationship stronger (Tonidandel, Avery, and Phillips 2007) and improve relational trust (Berkovich 2018). A stronger, more trust-filled role model–aspirant relationship is one that is more likely to have an impact on the aspirant.

Especially relevant with political role models is the likelihood that citizens are looking up to political figures whom they do not know personally, though certainly that is not always true. However, if, as I expect, Americans are predominantly taking their cues from more distant political leaders whom they do not know, relational proximity is likely determined by the extent of their exposure to that role model. While field experiments with prolonged exposure to role models have shown evidence of efficacy in a slew of research environments (e.g., Beaman et al. 2012; Dee 2004; Silverman et al. 1983), brief exposures have shown role model effects, too (Lockwood, Jordan, and Kunda 2002; Lockwood and Kunda 1997; Shin, Levy, and London 2016). How well known the role model is to the aspirant is an important consideration, as evidenced by the emphasis on research on parents, grandparents, and teachers as role models in children's lives (Coto et al. 2019; Dee 2004; Dunifon 2013; Holmes 1993; Lumpkin 2008;

Wiese and Freund 2011). These individuals are well known to children and thus are positioned to make a larger impact on them.

And so, ICT anticipates the importance of how known a political role model is to a citizen who admires them. A figure to whom an individual is routinely and/or frequently exposed will represent a closer political role model relationship and thus will have not only the potential to influence more strongly but the enhanced opportunity to do so as well.

ICT, in sum, suggests that some Americans will have political role models. Depending on how accessible those role models are, how persistent the connection with them is, and how closely they are known, they have the potential to influence political behavior and attitudes among those who have that connection—as the MTRM would predict. For many, those role models may be someone who shares important aspects of their identity. For those individuals, ICT anticipates that the impact of these role models will be to bolster what might otherwise be a sense of marginalization in politics—as the SIM would predict.

Conclusion

Psychology offers substantial insight into how and why individuals respond to the role models in their lives. We understand that human behavior is largely molded by socialization processes that promote social learning. Psychologists have established how even the most modest of interventions designed to inspire performance appear to motivate behavior change in a host of domains. Role models offer the possibility of motivating behavior that individuals might otherwise not aspire to. We also have a plethora of evidence that role models, when strategically used, can aid in mitigating inequities that exist around race, gender, class, and other factors and intersections that are associated with underrepresentation in areas from business to academia. Role models, then, are also protective against stereotypes that might demotivate individuals from behaving in certain ways.

This idea holds promise for our understanding of who engages with the U.S. political system and how various people might do so. The political psychology theory proposed in this book, ICT, integrates both MTRM and SIM into a unified theory for political role models by considering motivational processes for political participation as well as how those marginalized within politics can be moved to greater participation and engagement in a process they have historically been comparatively shut out of. As I reveal in Chapter 3, this integration is needed in how political science understands the existence and use of role models.

Political science has done little to address the themes associated with MTRM but instead aligns quite well with SIM. Both theories are crucial to our understanding of *when* role model effects occur and *how* these effects work. In Chapter 3, I discuss the significant body of literature in political science that discusses how important having someone who embodies your own traits—descriptive representation—is to an understanding of political efficacy and participation. Specifically, I outline the existing research on how the presence of role models impacts various forms of political participation and encourages those who have not historically been meaningfully integrated into American politics.

3

Role Models in Political Science

And to all the women, and especially the young women, who put their faith in this campaign and in me, I want you to know that nothing has made me prouder than to be your champion. Now, I—I know—I know we have still not shattered that highest and hardest glass ceiling, but some day someone will and hopefully sooner than we might think right now. And—and to all the little girls who are watching this, never doubt that you are valuable and powerful and deserving of every chance and opportunity in the world to pursue and achieve your own dreams.

—Democratic presidential nominee Hillary Clinton, November 9, 2016, concession speech

During the 2016 presidential campaign, Democrat Hillary Clinton frequently dug into the historical nature of her candidacy to present herself as a role model for other women and, in particular, young girls. When Clinton lost the race—which had been marked by misogyny on multiple fronts—political scientists David Campbell and Christina Wolbrecht (2020) found adolescent girls who also identified as Democrats to be disillusioned about politics. These girls were, however, also inspired to be more politically engaged, as witnessed by the countless numbers of them who participated in the Women's Marches that followed the inauguration of Clinton's rival, Donald Trump. This represents a change in behavior for only Democratic girls that was further encouraged by parental activism post-2016, offering additional evidence of a political role model effect—this time in the home (Campbell and Wolbrecht 2020).

As Chapter 2 outlines, research in social psychology has offered two primary and complementary theories into the (frequently positive, but not exclusively so) impact of role models on human behavior. Scholars in political science have offered an analysis of the impact of Clinton's historic run and more generally the impact of modeling on political engagement.

Neither political scientists nor psychologists, though, have drawn on either MTRM or SIM to offer any analysis of how the political landscape might be shaped in the wake of the first female nominee for the U.S. presidency.

In this chapter, I provide an overview of what political science has demonstrated about the impact of role models in two ways: role model effects and descriptive representation. In providing a background of the understanding of these two phenomena in political science, it is important that I carefully define the differences and the relationship between these two frequently intertwined (and perhaps confused) concepts. Role models, as I discuss in depth in Chapter 2, socialize others by modeling appropriate or preferred behavior. In a political context, that means they actively demonstrate engagement in and attitudes toward the political system. Others may aspire to and emulate these thoughts and actions. A role model may, for example, be an activist who speaks up against an emergent issue in the local community, thus illuminating a path for others to take action too. MTRM would govern how we might think about these effects, exploring the impact role models have on motivating others to participate in politics. Crucial to any motivating power, however, is that the aspirant either consciously or unconsciously recognizes this person as a role model.

In practice, people often look to role models whose identity provokes a connection. Conventional wisdom would suggest, and research in the vein of SIM confirms, that there are good reasons many of these political role models share significant markers of identity with aspirants. A shared life experience that may be presumed to come with similar backgrounds or demographics prompts aspirants to feel a greater sense of connection. In politics, in the abstract, this takes the form of descriptive representation, when an elected representative shares traits with those they represent and thus—presumably—may represent their interests too. Scholars have extended the consideration of potential effects of descriptive representation (i.e., seeing those who "look like you" in politics) to consider how this might also encourage political behavior. This research, to the best I can discern, focuses exclusively on those who have been otherwise marginalized in politics. That is, we compare everyone to the modal participant—older, white, male, cisgender, heterosexual, probably educated, and probably relatively wealthy.

A crucial distinction exists here. Political science has blurred the distinction between role model effects and descriptive representation. Frequently, scholars have analyzed the effect of the mere presence of a potential role model—Hillary Clinton being a good example—on behavior and attitudes. The potential role model may in fact be a role model to some of the population, but without individuals recognizing that person (again, either consciously or subconsciously) as a role model, that person is merely serving a representative role. If there is a match along some line of identity, that role is descriptive representation. Descriptive representation has a host of potentially positive influences on the citizenry. But if individuals are ignorant of that person's presence, do not acknowledge their presence, or reject their status as a potential role model, then there is no capacity for role model effects. Much of what political science has suggested to date about the presence of potential role models has not been genuinely tested for role model effects because individuals have not been asked whether they recognize a person (or people) as a political role model. Indeed, these effects are more aptly the impact of descriptive representation.

In this chapter, I draw on research that discusses both descriptive representation and role modeling to first outline what we know about how mass and elite populations appear to respond to role models and reveal the gaps in our understanding. We must keep in mind, of course, that in my social psychology conception of role models, they are conceptually and operationally different from descriptive representation. In this review I include role model effects in political science that are more accurately effects resulting from descriptive representation. Once I have reviewed this area of American politics literature, I then discuss what ICT can help us further understand about American political engagement.

Socialization

While, with this book, I am the first in political science to tackle how role models impact political participation using psychological theory, the field has provided a solid foundation for understanding political behavior more generally. Political behavior is a form of human behavior and is thus subject to many of the same cognitive processes as other behaviors. Political socialization is "the process by which people acquire relatively enduring political orientations toward politics in general and toward their own political systems" (Merelman 1986, 279) as well as how norms and practices are transferred to citizens, residents, and members (Sapiro 2004). This naturally includes how citizens view their social roles as part of their political environment.

Like other forms of socialization, political socialization begins in youth, as families and parents are a primary source of early socialization (Greenstein 1970; Davies 1965). As children age and spend less time with their families, other sources include school environments, peer groups, media, political institutions, community and religious organizations, and the military (Beck 1977; Marshall 1998). As such, this research has focused almost exclusively on preadolescents (Jennings 2007). This body of scholarship reveals that children are more likely to grow up to be active, informed, engaged citizens if they receive quality civic education in their youth (Andolina, Keeter et al. 2003; Langton and Jennings 1968; Niemi and Junn 1998); that voluntary group associations (e.g., student government) are associated with the development of skills that facilitate more meaningful participation (Campbell 2010; Smith 1999; Stolle and Hooghe 2004; Jennings and Stoker 2004); and that youth community service programs have the potential to encourage positive political values (Galston 2001; Niemi, Hepburn, and Chapman 2000).

While youth is, indeed, a crucial time for the development of future political dispositions, there are a multitude of ways that experiences, exposures, and contexts can shape an individual's political behavior. Among numerous other life contexts, social mobility (Walsh, Jennings, and Stoker 2004), marriage (Stoker and Jennings 1995), age, and education (Raaijmakers, Verbogt, and Vollebergh 1998) can impact an individual's political attitudes or behavior. For instance, it is easy to imagine that if our life partner is more politically active than we are, it might—over time—model more political engagement for us as well.

Cohort socialization effects are also well documented. Putnam (2000) illustrates how relatively civically engaged America's Baby Boomers have been. Verba, Schlozman, and Burns (2005) found that African Americans who transitioned to adulthood during the civil rights era were much more likely to be politically active as adults. More recently, focusing on attitudes around COVID-19 restrictions and threats, Deckman and her colleagues (2020) have documented notable ways that generational cohort interacted with gender to foster participation.

Implicit to this discussion of socialization both inside and outside the home and/or family of origin is that these effects are driven by the modeling of political behavior. Children develop an interest in politics (or do not) in part because of the exposure their caretakers provide when they are very young. Young adults take to the streets to protest injustices (or do not) in part because others in their community normalize (or do not) protest. Clearly, role models are doing some heavy lifting in the encouraging and discouraging of political behavior.

Role Models

The somewhat limited research that speaks directly to specific types of political role models is quite fragmented and rarely integrates findings from one type to the other. There are roughly four categories of this research: parents, teachers, celebrities, and political figures. I discuss each of these briefly here.

Parents

In large part because of the function parents serve in youth socialization, role model research in numerous country contexts is focused on parents and the impact they may have on their children's future political participation. Many of these studies (and others discussed here) do not explicitly use the term "role models" but rather consider these individuals as agents of socialization, especially for young people. This seems primarily a semantic distinction since the form and function are the same, though it could be argued that the subjects in these studies are not explicitly identifying these role models as such. However, it is also true that in virtually all extant research on role models, the aspirants are not identifying the role models, the researchers are.

Greater parental civic engagement and political participation are associated with greater engagement in their children (Andolina, Jenkins et al. 2003; Cicognani et al. 2012). In one study, the researchers found that young adults who had grown up in a home where there was frequent political discussion were 18 percent more likely to vote than those for whom there was no political discussion (Andolina, Jenkins et al. 2003). And, in a large study in Italy, a mother's participation was more significant, and these effects neutralized those of educational disparities (Dotti Sani and Quaranta 2015), a common and large predictor of whether or not someone votes. In Finland, researchers also found differences in engagement later in life based on the educational level of parents, but their parents' voting behavior was much more predictive of whether young people became voters themselves (Gidengil, Wass, and Valaste 2016). In other words, if parents vote, their kids are likely to be voters, too, and here again, mothers are the more potent role model (Oswald and Schmid 1998). Political efficacy and alienation also appear to be transmitted within the immediate family (Gniewosz, Noack, and Buhl 2009).

The most obvious connection between parental participation and that of their offspring is in children who run for political office. In Flanders, more than half of the candidates for political office had parents who were members of a Flemish political party (Wauters and Liefferinge 2017).[1] In the United States, Lawless and Fox (2005) found that among those most likely to run for office, having parents who discussed politics with them was a significant contributor to their interest in running for office. Of course,

Americans are also quite accustomed to the children of politicians running for office themselves (e.g., Bush, Kennedy), another factor that has been linked to candidate emergence (Lawless and Fox 2015).

These generational connections between civic behavior and political interest run deep, perhaps extending beyond one's immediate parental environment. In one study, individuals' likelihood of voting was tied not only to their own parents' behavior but also to their grandparents' political participation. That is, grandchildren are less likely to vote as adults if their grandparents did not vote; this is in large part because nonvoting grandparents are associated with nonvoting parents, thus increasing the odds that the third generation will also be nonvoters (Gidengil et al. 2020).

These parental effects appear to be even more important for girls' future political engagement in large part because socialization is a gendered process. As Bos et al. (2021) describe in developing their theoretical framework of gendered political socialization, boys and girls are subject to different socialization processes around both gender norms and roles and their appropriate connection to the political environment. As such, Bos and her colleagues have documented a host of gender-based differences in early childhood, gaps that continue and expand into adulthood and likely contribute to numerous gaps in political interest, participation, and representation that are well documented.

These gaps may be difficult to overcome, but there is some evidence that parents play an important role in encouraging girls to think about their engagement differently. In the aftermath of the 2016 U.S. presidential election, Campbell and Wolbrecht (2020) have been evaluating the impact of a very "gender-charged" political environment on the nation's girls. They found that in 2016, adolescent political attitudes and participation were strongly correlated to how their parents modeled attitudes (i.e., disillusionment) and participation (i.e., protest), regardless of gender. But what they have found since is that Democratic girls, in particular, have undergone significant changes in their anticipated or intended political engagement. It is not difficult to imagine that moms all over the country (and really, the world) were setting an example for their left-leaning daughters by participating in and taking them to the Women's March and other political events.

Teachers

Given their importance during children's formative years, teachers are well positioned to serve as role models as well, political and otherwise. Andolini, Keeter et al. (2003) found that nearly half of high school students

(48 percent) who had taken a course with a civic component were more interested in political issues after taking the class. The same was true for college students (47 percent), though fewer of them took courses with this type of content. More specifically, teachers who modeled sustainable behaviors—that are now seen by many as political acts—like recycling or using green transit options encouraged their students to do so, too (Higgs and McMillan 2006).

However, while teachers are well positioned to influence students during their formative years, students do not actually tend to recognize them as political role models (Bricheno and Thornton 2007; Bromnick and Swallow 1999). It is, of course, possible that students are taking these exemplars for granted in reporting their role models and that there is active modeling going on subconsciously, but the lack of acknowledgment of teachers by their students is consistent with findings in psychology that show students rarely consciously acknowledge their teachers as role models.

For college students, role models are more relevant because their professors are often professionals or experts in the fields they aspire to. Especially when there is a stereotype threat involved in the career choice, like women in STEM or men in teaching, ingroup role models can be highly relevant and helpful (Lockwood 2006). When it comes to politics, however, the predominant conversation about "modeling" in higher education is really a discussion of the potential for indoctrination on political values. If political indoctrination is taking place in college classrooms, this could be considered a role model effect.

Political scientists are familiar with this argument (see Giersch 2020) since we tend to be the figurative tip of this spear. Anecdotally, the joke is that we cannot even reliably get students to read their syllabi let alone influence political attitudes. American college faculty are somewhat more politically liberal than the general population, which has invited concerns about indoctrination among conservatives (Bloom 1987; Buckley 1951; Horowitz 2010; Shapiro 2010) and the media (Friedersdorf 2012; Shields and Dunn 2016; Wooldridge 2005) for many years. Research, however, mostly disputes these claims because university faculty are more politically diverse and less radical than they may be portrayed (Gross and Simmons 2014) and, importantly, faculty ideology has almost no effect on student ideology (Kelly-Woessner and Woessner 2008; Mariani and Hewitt 2008). So, while teachers, and later professors, can serve as role models for many behaviors—and school, and later college, can definitely be a politically formative experience (see Longo and Meyer 2006 for a review)—it does not appear that there is much of a role model effect impacting political attitudes or behavior.

Celebrities

What about Oprah? Do celebrities—as otherwise nonpolitical yet high-profile figures—influence political behavior and attitudes by modeling for the American public? Available research on celebrities' importance in electoral political engagement in the United States offers an inconclusive picture. Some studies show that members of the U.S. electorate generally show strong support for a favored celebrity's political issue campaign, but these attitudes may not translate to a change in substantive political participation shown through actions like voting or running for office (Majic, O'Neill, and Bernhard 2020 for an overview).

Despite this apparent gap between celebrities' impacts on political attitudes and political participation, it is important to note that celebrities are uniquely well positioned to possess sociocultural and political power to promote change from their status as elite, non-state agents (Driessens 2013; Gunter 2014; Rojek 2015). This influence also allows individuals with this type of fame to use their existing platform to cleverly merge consumption of endorsed products with "peace and development," reinforcing practices that attempt to sell the average person a solution to sociopolitical issues (Budabin 2020, 1).

The celebrity is a special type of expert, "whose knowledge is not derived from numbers, deduction, or semi-structured interviews, but from 'feeling the pain' of the poor and from offering an emotional connection to the subjects of development" (Budabin 2019, 3). This is how celebrities, like U2's Bono, craft well-endowed charity campaigns, like the Make Poverty History campaign in the Global South or Ben Affleck and George Clooney's Brand Aid campaigns boasting the benefits of sustainable coffee with the goal to raise money to help those in the Global South and Africa (Budabin 2020).[2] Therefore, celebrities' influence as political role models may not always be the most effective in crafting policy change, as they lack direct experience in crafting solutions and do not have accountability to the causes for which they are advocating, leaving them removed from the issues they claim to represent and therefore poorly equipped to suggest meaningful solutions (Budabin 2020; Choi and Berger 2010). Relatedly, as technological advancement makes it easier for celebrities to participate in global politics by utilizing social media as a tool to rally wider audiences, they have also increasingly participated in domestic legislative processes in the United States. Studies appear to show that celebrities' testimonies on certain political issues may not ultimately create change by themselves (Biccum 2011). Celebrities have the *potential* to exert considerable influence over democratic and legislative processes. However, existing research calls into question whether potential celebrity influence as political role models can be translated into substantive political participation (Becker 2013; Majic, O'Neill, and Bernhard 2020; Vesey 2015).

In terms of translating political power to substantive political action, existing research is also mixed. Pease and Brewer (2008) tested the extent to which the "Oprah effect"—the media and cultural mogul's sizable social, economic, and political influence waged through product endorsements on anything from cars to books—could spur additional electoral support for her endorsed candidate, Barack Obama, for the Democratic presidential nomination in 2008. However, after study participants read different news stories about Winfrey's endorsement and answered questions regarding their opinions of Obama, there was not a noticeable attitudinal change in the participants regarding Obama. However, the authors found that reading the news on the endorsement "did lead participants to see Obama as more likely to win the nomination and to say that they would be more likely to vote for him" (386), but whether this greater likelihood resulted in increased voter turnout for Obama was not clear (Majic, O'Neill, and Bernhard 2020; Pease and Brewer 2008).

Additionally, Frizzell (2011) finds that even political messaging from high-profile celebrity activists like Bono is neither well believed nor acted upon by most study participants because celebrities are not a trusted source. This study also suggests that Republicans and independents are less likely than Democrats to adhere to the political issue position of a celebrity, as they perceived celebrities as holding more liberal political beliefs, thereby discrediting them. Celebrities tend to identify more with liberal positions, which could mean that the extent to which celebrities have political influence as role models could depend on a given person's party ideology or other personal identities such as race, class, or gender. Taken together, these studies illustrate that while celebrities have the potential to serve as role models and have significant influence due to their fame, notoriety, and monetary capital, their endorsement of a certain political action or ideology may nonetheless not be trusted in the same way that their endorsement of a product or service may be (Majic, O'Neill, and Bernhard 2020). Therefore, the electorate's likelihood of aspiring to a celebrity's political attitudes, preferences, or behaviors may change depending on identity-based factors like party identification or whether the individual celebrity is considered a credible source of information (Nisbett and DeWalt 2016).

Jackson (2008) finds young people are significantly more likely than older generations to agree with a position held by a celebrity. Nonetheless, celebrity status is not necessarily a determinant in influencing public opinion; rather, celebrities whom youth voters deem credible and who hold similar values have the greatest likelihood of influencing youth public opinion—which researchers like Addis (1996) would consider a role modeling effect. These findings illustrate that if a celebrity embodies a particular set of aspirations and possesses a generally high level of political or informational credibility, this intersection can create cues for the youngest segment of the electorate.

In addition to youth, race and sexual orientation appear to predict aspirational political engagement. For example, Lady Gaga's song "Born This Way" shifted public opinion toward acceptance of genetic explanations of homosexuality. Followers of Gaga's social media, where she regularly discussed LGBTQ+ issues and causes, were reportedly more politically engaged than those who did not follow her (Click, Lee, and Holladay 2017; Jang and Lee 2014). Similarly, Beyoncé and Nicki Minaj's powerful Black girl magic anthem "Feelin' Myself" was found to have an indelible impact on young Black women's self-image, allowing them to see "parts of themselves, be it aspirational or functional . . . in which they could express the joys of being a Black woman" and helped them feel empowered to participate in activism, especially online (Halliday and Brown 2018, 233).

Colin Kaepernick, the former NFL player, is another celebrity who has spurred political action. Towler, Crawford, and Bennett (2020) examine how Black Americans have been mobilized by Kaepernick's activism, protest against police violence, and support of the Black Lives Matter movement. Black Americans who support Kaepernick's activism are more likely to partake in nontraditional, individual-level forms of political engagement such as grassroots activism, illustrating that ingroup identification among this demographic is strong and that "Black celebrity interaction has the potential to mobilize Black Americans to political action" (Towler, Crawford, and Bennett 2020, 122). Those with a strong sense of ingroup identity or feelings of identity disenfranchisement can look for high-profile figures who advocate in ways traditional politicians may not. Celebrities who embody the appropriate values, are credible, and regularly utilize their platforms to discuss issues may actively help certain demographics to engage more with politics.

Researchers are still determining how President Donald Trump fits this celebrity profile, as well as his impact as a political role model. However, it is clear that his campaign for and subsequent term as president was politically mobilizing for those with shared ingroup identities. Namely, he cultivated white Christians of lower socioeconomic status, who feared progressivism as a threat to American security, as his voting base (Homolar and Scholz 2019; Whitehead, Perry, and Baker 2018). Some argue that

Trump's celebrity status, where he acted as the "star" of his own show of American politics (Street 2019), helped him effectively mobilize a loyal fan base and turn them into fans rather than supporters. This, in turn, made it easier for him to convince his voting base that any change that came from any other politician than Trump himself would destroy American ideas and lifestyle (Homolar and Scholz 2019). In this way, Trump used his notoriety as a celebrity and his charismatic personality to create a swath of loyal fans who aspired to be like him, looked up to him, and—in some cases—believed he was sent by God to save them (Hassan 2020, Homolar and Scholz 2019). Majic, O'Neill, and Bernhard (2020) argue this situation is potentially dangerous to American democracy. Trump used his limited experience in politics to gain widespread approval for initiatives that might not be the most effective in solving those exact complex issues and won on those promises.

His lack of experience in governing aside, Trump has also been repetitively accused of racial, ethnic, and gender prejudice throughout his time as a celebrity figurehead and during his time in office. Notably, since his election in 2016, many have additionally found evidence that both self-reported and observable racial prejudice are more prevalent in his supporters than in those who supported Hilary Clinton (Fitzduff 2017; Giani and Méon 2021; Green and McElwee 2019; Hooghe and Dassonneville 2018). For example, a study by Green and McElwee (2019) found that the biggest determinant of support for Trump was biased racial attitudes. Furthermore, after President Trump was elected, not only did self-reported racial resentment more than double in survey respondents, but anti-Latinx microaggressions among students increased on college campuses and hate crime rates against this ethnic group increased by upward of 10 percent. Quality of life for Black Americans has decreased since Trump took office in 2016, and hate crimes, especially against racial and ethnic minority groups, have been steadily increasing over the same time period (Clayton, Moore, and Jones-Eversley 2019; Giani and Méon 2019; Hassan 2019). This, along with anecdotal evidence, reveals that Trump, a well-known celebrity long before his presidential campaign, did seem to model behaviors that were emulated in the electorate following his election as U.S. president.

While Donald Trump is one of the most recent examples of successful celebrities-turned-political-candidates, the historical prevalence of celebrities like Arnold Schwarzenegger and Ronald Reagan points to the potential for high-profile linkages between celebrities' political participation and role model effects in the electorate.

Political Figures

Of course, most obviously, political role models may also be political figures. In political science, discussion of political role models and their impact has evolved mostly connected to the concept of descriptive representation. As I have already alluded to, the problem with this connection is that these concepts (role model effects and descriptive representation) are not necessarily one and the same, and presumably the impacts may be different. Descriptive representation includes role model effects, but not all role models are descriptive, and in realms where there are few or no potential role models, descriptive representation may be unlikely or even impossible. Another possibility is the role model may actually have to be more distant or tangential in order to inspire. Furthermore, it is not clear that those being descriptively represented are even aware of the presence of the potential role model, all but certainly creating a scenario where there would be no impact of their presence.

As such, all this political science literature on role models is in the vein of SIM, in which those who are like us in politics have the potential to encourage us to also participate in politics, perhaps despite other obstacles we might face. There is little to no research that is strictly in the spirit of MTRM—research that would just strictly identify the mere presence and impact of a role model or role models on political attitudes and behavior. This is more than a semantic consideration. Role models do not necessarily have to share our traits to inspire us to engage in politics (though they often do), but you would not know that by reading the extant literature on role models.

Consider a significant example from contemporary politics. An NPR headline from March 2017 read, "On Both the Left and Right, Trump Is Driving New Political Engagement." The story reveals how, on the Left, President Trump inspired progressive activism to unforeseen levels in American politics. On the Right, Trump routinely brought tens of thousands out to his rallies. As Tufts University sociologist Sarah Sobeiraj told NPR for the story:

> Saying those things and acting that way brought people out because they felt validated by someone who sees the world the way they see it, feeling at last as though someone was really telling the truth without apology. And on the left, that way of speaking was absolutely objectionable and mobilizing, because they were viewed as abhorrent. (quoted in Sydell 2017)

In its literal sense, descriptive representation does not have much explanatory power here. Trump is an older, wealthy, white man who attended elite schools his entire life and experienced none of the hardships everyday Americans face, unlike virtually all of his supporters and detractors. Nonetheless, the man served—in dramatic fashion—as both a positive and negative role model for millions of Americans who suddenly found themselves interested in engaging in politics.

Descriptive Representation

Trump did, however, attempt to cultivate a sense of shared identity with his supporters, and it is the idea of "linked fate" (Weller and Junn 2018) that has been associated with higher levels of political participation among white people (Berry, Ebner, and Cornelius 2019). This, symbolically at least, hints at how descriptive representation may be leveraged in role model effects.

The majority of what political scientists have contributed to our understanding of the impact political role models have on the political landscape has been generated by drawing on theories of descriptive representation, or the idea of one individual symbolically "standing for" another (Pitkin 1967, 92). Descriptive representation is, as Jane Mansbridge (1999) described, "individuals who in their own backgrounds mirror some of the more frequent experiences and outward manifestations of belonging to the group" (628). The theoretical argument on behalf of descriptive representation is that when individuals playing key roles in government share a lived experience with those they represent, individuals will have more positive feelings toward government and perhaps democratic governance will be more reflective of the needs and desires of its citizenry.

Descriptive representation is inherently linked to political role models in that this model of representation is executed by those citizens that feel some connection to because of shared experiences or identities. As such, research on the impact of role models has been through an aggregated lens of their existence in the form of descriptive representation. Most of this research has been focused on how the presence of women may impact those who identify as women or girls. Presumably there would be similar expectations for other identities since other fields have examined a host of marginalized identities, but political science has been slow to examine these.

A natural experiment in India offers some of the clearest evidence of the potential for role model effects. In 1993, a national law instituted gender quotas for elected positions on India's village councils and implemented them randomly, leading to dramatically higher local political representation for women in the country. Researchers suspected the sudden presence of so many more women to serve as potential political role models might be associated with how girls—and their parents—in those villages viewed their futures.

As Beaman et al. (2012) reveal, parents in India continue to have more ambitious aspirations for their male children regardless of the makeup of the political leadership in their village. However, the gap between aspirations for boy children and those for girl children has closed substantially in villages with more female leadership. The same is true for future expectations of the girls themselves. In villages with quotas for women, girls were more likely to want to get an education, work outside their home, and choose their own career path—among other expectations that push at traditional gender roles. This research offers conclusive evidence that women's presence in politics serves to influence the perceptions and behavior of others.

It should be noted that for most of U.S. history, this was not even a question that could be studied systematically; there were just too few women, people of color, people with disabilities, or those who were openly LGBT (let alone QIA+)—or even those from lower economic status—in public view to serve as role models. Starting in the early 1990s, women's representation became less rare. And following the so-called Year of the Woman in 1992, women also became more visible in politics. At that time there were a number of high-profile governors, such as Governor Ann Richards in Texas (1991–1995), and two women sent to the U.S. Senate by the same state (California, Democrats Barbara Boxer and Dianne Feinstein), joining a handful of other women and a growing contingent in the House of Representatives.

With women becoming a more obvious presence in politics, researchers could begin to look at the impacts of their participation. By definition, political socialization has its most profound impact when it changes how younger people think about their place in a political system. Politically active parents—particularly mothers—helped encourage greater political interest in their adult daughters in a sample of English-speaking Canadians (Gidengil, O'Neill, and Young 2010). Scholars thus justifiably focused some of this initial attention on how young people respond to descriptive representation.

Campbell and Wolbrecht (2006) were the first to ask whether young women who were exposed to a high-profile woman in politics were more likely to show interest in political activism. They found that visibility of women and their campaigns in the media was likely encouraging families to talk more about politics, which, in turn, appeared to foster greater intent to be politically active among adolescent girls. Essentially, women playing an enhanced role in politics prompted girls to pay more attention and consider their own contribution more fully, too (Campbell and Wolbrecht 2006).

These positive effects hold true for women and girls across a number of country contexts as well. Wolbrecht and Campbell (2007) found that the presence of women in three parliaments is associated with more political discussion and political participation among women. Their presence had an even more potent impact on discussions and plans for participation among adolescent girls. A larger study of 35 national legislatures also found both women and men were more likely to have positive attitudes about politics where there were more elected women (Karp and Banducci 2008). The potential to engage women more deeply in politics is not necessarily even limited to role model effects in democracies (Schuler 2019). In the United States, however, these positive effects on the interest and participation of girls seem, so far, to have been limited by ideology and party (Mariani, Marshal, and Mathews-Schultz 2015).

Less conclusive, however, is whether women's descriptive representation is associated with candidate emergence of women. Outside the U.S. context, some analyses found that the presence of elected women temporarily boosts the number of women running for office (Gilardi 2015), while others document a longer-lasting correlation (Beaman et al. 2009, 2012; Bhavnani 2008; Deininger and Liu 2013). This type of inquiry is relatively new in the United States, and it has been less conclusive. Using a large dataset of more than 3,800 observations, Broockman (2014) found null effects—an increase in the number of elected women is not associated with any increase in women's political participation. Ladam, Harden, and Windett (2018), however, limit their analyses to only prominent women officeholders, seemingly recognizing that descriptive representation alone is not a sufficient condition for role model effects. These scholars did find a substantially positive relationship—an increase of about 3 percent or so—between the presence of women officeholders and more women candidates for state legislative office.

Experimental work on role models also exists, but creating a role model treatment that is meaningful enough to change political attitudes or modify political behavior is understandably a challenge. Brief exposure to a researcher-generated role model seems to yield no impact (Foos and Gilardi 2020; Schneider and Holman 2020), though a more substantial exposure to a respondent-identified one did have modest effects (Sweet-Cushman 2018a).

Individual Impacts

Again, this research primarily examines women's political attitudes and behavior. We do not know how men or those with multiple relevant identities respond to the presence of role models, descriptive or not. There is also relatively little investigation of the individual impacts of self-identified role models on political attitudes or behavior in large part because it is more difficult to disaggregate the impact of descriptive representation.

An exception to this gap is a relatively small study I conducted in 2017 (Sweet-Cushman 2018a) with participants attending a nonpartisan campaign training designed for women that specifically employed the use of role models. In this study, the attendees were asked to identify someone they had been exposed to during the training whom they identified as a role model. There was a correlation between those who strongly identified with the role model they selected and higher political ambition. This study also revealed some preliminary evidence that female role models exhibiting counterstereotypical traits are more effective in encouraging women to think concretely about running for office. I rely on this study more fully to answer questions central to this book in Chapter 7.

What Inspired Citizenship Theory Can Tell Us: Expectations

We know role models can play a part in the political socialization and behavior of Americans and that this impact might be particularly important for those who identify as women. But this leaves us with a host of other questions about the role these exemplars play in shaping American politics and citizenship. In the chapters that follow, I explore some of these unexplored questions about "inspired citizenship": positive political attitudes, participation, and candidate emergence.

Virtually all examinations of political role models have been researcher driven—that is, the researcher identified the individuals who would normatively seem to be in a position to be a role model (but see Sweet-Cushman 2018a). While there are plenty of reasons to consider those strategically positioned to serve as role models, role modeling is inherently a very individualized experience. Aspirants may feel no connection to someone a researcher identifies but may feel a connection to someone they self-identify with in a way that is meaningful. As such, my first effort is to identify whom Americans in general (Chapter 4), and especially those who run for political office (Chapter 5), identify as their political role models. We should, for example, anticipate that role model effects have the potential to serve different purposes for political elites than for those in the general public who have a more casual relationship with American democracy. In the chapters that follow, I examine the impact of role models in both populations to establish who the identified role models are and what their relationships are to the aspirants.

In keeping with an ICT theoretical framework that integrates MTRM and SIM, there should be patterns visible in the role models identified. First, we should expect that there will be a broad range of people identified as role models by individuals. Some people will likely identify high-profile individuals, some of whom have been included in extant research of role models, like former secretary of state Hillary Clinton (D-NY). Other aspirants may identify close personal connections who have modeled political behavior or attitudes. Personally, high-profile women politicians like Vice President Kamala Harris (D-CA) and Senator Kay Bailey Hutchinson (R-TX) have always inspired me to participate in politics and have cultivated positive attitudes toward politics and government, but my life is also rich with examples of politically active acquaintances and friends who have modeled more tangible political acts and would constitute political role models as well. As MTRM would suggest, either example could prove a fruitful role model in the political realm. Either a proximal or a distal relationship could provide potent political modeling if the relationship is conducive. Indeed, the "relationship" could be mutual, or the aspirant might just admire the political role model from afar through the media. However, deep positive relationships are always apt to bear more fruit—in this case, because they provide a deeper insight into the behavior and attitudes that can be modeled. As such, I predict the following:

> *Inspired Citizenship Motivation Prediction:* The deeper the connection with a positive political role model, the more likely an individual is to hold positive citizenship values and participate actively in political citizenship activities.

As evident in the analyses I conduct in Chapters 4 through 7, I operationalize "deeper connection" using three qualities of an aspirant–role model relationship, the role model orientation, that have been shown to be extremely relevant in the MTRM literature on role models. While there are perhaps others that could be included in examining these relationships, these three seem most relevant to relationships within a political context. I am most interested in the attainability of the role model's success (*attainability*), the closeness of the relationship to the role model (*known*), and how long the relationship with the role model has persisted (*duration*). These three features shape the motivational aspect of ICT.

The intensity of the role model connection is what—as Bandura (1986) might concur—puts the "teeth" in the impression about the target behavior (i.e., attention and retention). However, the specific qualities the role model possesses are more crucial in the reproduction and motivation of behavior as well as the reinforcement of the components of modeling. This is a largely unexplored area of research. Is it, perhaps, not just important who our role models are in politics but also what they are like? What they advocate? What their values are and how they communicate them? Self-identification with a role model likely presupposes a positive role model (negative role models could also be motivating), but what traits do these individuals have? Do they possess stereotypical traits, like strong leadership and charisma, common in politics (Bauer 2020; Schneider and Bos 2014; Sweet-Cushman 2020) or counterstereotypical ones? Preliminary research that I have conducted elsewhere (Sweet-Cushman 2018a) suggested that—for women considering a run for office—both stereotypical and counterstereotypical traits can be motivating, just in different ways. Given the dramatic diversity of the American public, and increasingly those who run for office, we would expect the same might apply more broadly, too. How Americans recognize these types of traits in their self-identified role models should be illuminating, especially in the context of different intersections of identity that existing scholarship has not addressed.

For many individuals, the connection with their professed role models may be provoked and strengthened by a shared identity, as is implied for women and girls in much of the extant literature on role models. But as SIM would suggest, there is likely a similar connection for others with politically marginalized identities. To draw on Jane Mansbridge's famous provocation (1999) around descriptive representation, "Should Blacks represent Blacks and women represent women?" this book aims to answer a more practical question—namely, *do Blacks inspire Blacks and women inspire women?* What about other identities, including those that are not or less so historically marginalized? SIM would suggest that ingroup role models have the potential to narrow or close identity-based gaps in political attitudes, participation, and candidate emergence. Where this marginalization has left some less engaged in the political process and feeling less positive (and potentially more negative) about American politics, an ingroup role model has the potential to level the playing field:

> *Inspired Citizenship Inoculation Prediction*: Individuals with ingroup role models will have enhanced positive political attitudes, participation, and candidate emergence compared to those who do not.

At the very least, ICT offers a way of looking at descriptive representation and role model effects as separate phenomenon at play in shaping political behavior and attitudes. A multifaceted empirical examination of the motivation and inoculation predictions and an accompanying analysis of role model traits should greatly expand our descriptive knowledge of how role models contribute to the healthy functioning of American democracy. It may also suggest ways we are not tapping into the potential of political role models or are tapping into negative aspects of role model effects. I turn to these questions for the American public en masse in Chapter 4.

4

Political Role Models and Everyday Jane

Following the violent protests on January 6, 2021, at Capitol Hill in Washington, D.C., Christopher Grider, a 39-year-old vineyard owner from Texas, was charged with seven counts ranging from destruction of government property and aiding and abetting to an act of physical violence (Shaw 2021). In an interview on Texas television following his participation in the riot, Grider clearly attributed the inspiration for his participation in the violent protest to outgoing president Donald Trump. "The president asked people to come and show their support," he said. "I feel like it's the least that we can do; it's kind of why I came from central Texas all the way to D.C." (quoted in Axon and Salman 2021). Many of those arrested for participation in the political-protests-turned-insurrection said the same. Indeed, less than a week after the attack on the Capitol, the House of Representatives brought and affirmed an article of impeachment against Trump for "incitement of insurrection" (U.S. Congress 2021).

While Trump was ultimately not convicted by the U.S. Senate of the charges put forth in the articles of impeachment, he continues to loom large over American politics. Whether it was in calling for "patriotic" protest on insurrection day (Naylor 2021) or hosting his infamous massive rallies during his presidential campaigns, there is a clear sense that Trump's emergence as a serious political figure has inspired a significant number of ordinary Americans to participate in politics in extraordinary ways. By definition, Donald Trump is a political role model.

Trump's candidacies and presidency inspired many theories about what was motivating his voters, many of whom had been previously disengaged from the political process (Morgan and Lee 2018). One of the first scholarly postmortems following the 2016 election evaluated the two most prevalent explanatory claims to emerge. The dominant narrative was that white working-class voters felt left behind during Obama-era prosperity and Trump's rhetoric exploited this insecurity. The second was that Trump used his campaign to stoke the flames of racism and sexism in the electorate (Schaffner, MacWilliams, and Nteta 2018). Both these explanations focus on his base, who were—on average—of lower socioeconomic status than those who supported Trump's challengers in both 2016 and 2020. Schaffner and his colleagues found that, despite the dominant narrative being around economic insecurity, sexism and especially racism played the most pivotal role in getting Trump voters to the polls.

This really was unsurprising given that less educated white people and a number of Trump-friendly religious groups tend to harbor more racism and sexism (Schuman et al. 1997; Glick and Friske 1996; Glick et al. 2002). However, these factors might also have predicted that these groups would be otherwise unlikely to participate in presidential politics. Higher levels of income and education are significant predictors of political participation (Leighly and Nagler 2013; Verba, Schlozman, and Brady 1995), though social capital built on the job, within religious institutions, or through volunteering can compensate for other detractors by helping build civic skills that enable participation (Brady, Verba, and Scholzman 1995; Djupe and Grant 2001; Farris and Holman 2014; Hays and Kogl 2007).

This is all to say that where there is low social capital, populism has the potential to thrive (Giuliano and Wacziarg 2020; Lynch et al. 2019), and populism loves nothing more than a charismatic populist out front encouraging people to engage in the cause. By definition *and in practice*, Donald Trump is a role model.

In this chapter, I use ICT to examine how Donald Trump, and the numerous other role models that everyday Americans report looking to for political inspiration, does and does not impact their political participation. I do this through the lens of the two predictions that frame this book. First, the *Inspired Citizenship Motivation Prediction* should mean that Americans who have political role models may have different attitudes (e.g., trust in government or political efficacy) and patterns of political participation (e.g., voting or contacting their elected officials) than those who do not have political role models. It also predicts that those with a stronger connection to their political role model will have stronger attitudes to and more engagement in American politics.

For those who have been historically marginalized from the world of politics, a role model with whom they share an identity should be particularly inspiring, as the *Inspired Citizenship Inoculation Prediction* posits. Americans with these marginalized identities should be aided in their connection to American politics by identifying (and especially identifying strongly) with an ingroup role model.

In this spirit, the following analyses identify whether Americans have political role models, who they are, what they are like, and what impact those connections (or lack thereof) have on their orientation toward the political aspects of their citizenship. In this chapter, as well as those that follow, I focus on a number of behaviors and attitudes that are central to the American civic experience. For average citizens, voting is the modal way (and often the only way) they may engage in the political process. Those who are more involved may act in other ways. I examine the more common forms of political participation and, where feasible, voting. I also examine a number of political attitudes that are important to civic life.

The use of these behaviors and attitudes as dependent variables provides just a sample of how citizens are provoked to be more deeply connected to civic and political life. Knowing more about how individuals connect to political role models can aid our understanding of the importance of role models in inspiring political participation and cultivating healthy relationships between citizens and their democratic system and institutions.

Data and Methods

I examine these relationships between Americans and their (potential) political role models using a survey of adult Americans ($n = 1,723$)[1] fielded in May 2021 using the Lucid Theorem, a respondent discovery platform that aids researchers in surveying nationally representative samples. Lucid directed their respondents to my survey, which was hosted on Qualtrics survey software. The survey asked respondents about their political attitudes and behavior as well as about their political role models. Lucid provides respondent demographic information.

For the just over 1,700 respondents who remained once the data was cleaned, demographic information, including race/ethnicity, gender, party, education, and region, was collected directly from respondents using Lucid Theorem. All regions in the United States were represented, with roughly 20 percent of the respondents from the Northeast, Midwest, and West and a notably higher concentration of respondents from the South (37.8 percent). The mean age was 47 years, and the vast majority of respondents had at least a high school education, with the highest percentage of this group (24.1) having obtained a bachelor's degree. There was an over-representation of women in the sample (57 percent), while 43 percent were men, and this group of respondents was racially and ethnically diverse as well. For example, while three-quarters of respondents identified as white (77.4 percent), the next highest respondent racial identification was Black or African American (9.9 percent), then Hispanic or Latinx American (4.3 percent) and some other race (2.7 percent).

Finally, politically, respondents to some degree identified more with either the Democratic Party or the Republican Party (only 10 percent were independents), and most respondents were strong partisans, with a combined total of nearly half (46.5 percent) reporting they were either strong Democrats or strong Republicans (26.9 and 19.6 percent, respectively). More moderate partisans (those who identified with a party but not as strongly as those who identified at the extremes of the scales) made up a slightly smaller 43.6 percent of the sample. This data also illustrates there were more Democratic respondents generally (47.4 percent) than Republicans (35.2 percent), and there were 7.3 percent more strong Democrats than Republicans—providing sufficient ideological variations within the group.

By way of comparison, this sample is not dissimilar from the one drawn for the American National Election Studies (ANES) survey, the gold standard for American political science, in 2020. Roughly 20 percent of ANES respondents also came from each of the four census regions, but with the same somewhat higher representation in the South (37.2 percent compared to my 37.8 percent). The mean age of ANES respondents was a modest little more than four years older, no doubt attributable to a methodology that better captures older respondents who might not be as likely to participate in web-based surveys. ANES also drew a similarly educated sample, with the modal education level attained also being a bachelor's degree (24.9 percent vs. 24.1 percent). The samples were also skewed female to almost exactly the same degree (57.3 percent ANES vs. my 57 percent). Racially, my sample was slightly more white (by about 4 percent) and Black (by 1 percent), but less Hispanic (by 5 percent).

Politically, Lucid assesses partisanship in a somewhat different way, but the differences are more in the number who identify as independents—which is itself a topic of debate in political science (Klar and Krupnikov 2016). Nonetheless, the ANES sample contains 43.7 percent Democrats compared to my somewhat larger 47.4 percent of the sample, but I have a higher percentage of Republicans (35.2 percent) than does the 2020 ANES (31.4 percent). In all, the sample used in this chapter is roughly as nationally representative as the most recent ANES.

Do Americans Identify with Political Role Models?

Of course, Americans have role models, and, as I discussed in Chapter 3, frequently they are celebrities, sports figures, teachers, or parents. We know these individuals have the capacity to influence political attitudes and behavior, too, but I wanted to know if Americans explicitly identify a political role model in their lives. And, if so, I wanted to know who these individuals are, what the relationship with them is like, and ultimately how these relationships are associated with how people feel about and participate in the American political system.

I first asked respondents if they identify with a political role model. Slightly more than half (52.1 percent) reported that there is at least one person they identify as a political role model.[2] Respondents who indicated they had a political role model were asked a number of additional questions about the role model whom they thought of as being most influential on them. One way that social psychology has demonstrated the potency of role models is by demonstrating their success and attainability (Lockwood and Kunda 1997). I thus measure—for those who report having a political role model—how they perceive these role models. I combine two questions (whether they could attain similar success and whether other people could reach this level of success) to form a scale variable of role model *attainability*.[3] I also calculate a role model *known/closeness* variable[4] given research that demonstrates that "superstar" role models are less effective (Lockwood and Kunda 1997) than those whose accomplishments are less overwhelming or threatening to one's own motivation or ambition (Tesser 1991; Tesser and Campbell 1983). I also include a measure of how long the aspirant has identified with the role model, role model *duration*, since I anticipate many respondents likely chose someone who had recently inspired them—which may be no less meaningful than a longer connection. In other words, I do not suspect it matters much to contemporary political engagement whether you have been inspired for a long time or relatively recently by a political role model.

In considering the motivational aspect of ICT, I consider how having a role model and these three relational considerations (attainability, closeness, and duration) for modeling contribute to political behavior (voting and other political acts) and attitudes (trust, efficacy, aggression, etc.). I include other variables frequently shown to contribute to political engagement (race, education, gender, political interest, etc.)[5] in these models. ICT would predict that those with political role models, especially successful role models who are seen as modeling attainable political behavior and are close to the aspirant, will be more politically active and have more positive attitudes toward politics.

Role Models Inspiring Political Behavior

At least subconsciously, political campaigns seem to appreciate the impact a role model could have on the electorate. At higher levels (e.g., presidential campaigns), campaigns frequently deploy high-profile, popular surrogates for the candidate to help with get-out-the-vote efforts. These potential role models are attempting to mobilize voters to turn out on election day by using their status to inspire people who presumably feel a connection to them. For example, in 2016 the Clinton campaign famously brought former president Barack Obama to Philadelphia—a city whose turnout was pivotal in winning crucial Pennsylvania—for a massive rally on the eve of the election. In Philly, known for its fondness of booing (Graham 2016), Obama repeated his now iconic exhortation, "Don't boo, vote." The Clinton campaign was banking on Obama being someone who could model behavior for the voters they needed to turn out.

The most common way citizens will ever participate in American democracy across their lifetime is by casting a vote for president. However, it is common for only about half or a bit more of eligible adults to participate in these elections, and midterm and local elections have even less participation. ICT suggests that those who feel connected to a political role model would feel more invested in the political system and may be motivated to participate in American politics at higher rates than those who do not identify with a political role model. Thus, I first look at this most common form of participation to see if these differences exist.

I ask respondents to self-report whether they voted in the 2020 presidential election, the most recent major general election most respondents would have had an opportunity to participate in. Fully 80 percent of the sample reported voting in the election. Admittedly this high participation rate is suspect, but not unexpectedly so. Countless scholarly endeavors have revealed the social desirability bias that impacts self-reports of voting behavior (Andolina, Keeter et al. 2003; Brockington and Karp 2002; Corbett 1991; Holbrook and Krosnick 2010; Lutz 2003; Lyons and Scheb 1999), with nonvoters claiming to have voted out of shame or embarrassment for not having gone to the polls. Nonetheless, for my purposes, that built-in error at the very least represents a population of nonvoters who recognize that there may be some normative value in voting. More importantly, there are somewhat large and statistically significant ($p < .001$) differences in these reported voting rates of those with role models (86 percent) and those without (74.7 percent). This pattern, however, does not hold up in multivariate analysis when controlling for other factors like political interest and age are more likely to be associated with voting and having a political role model or, for those with role models, features of that role model do not reach statistical significance. Neither *attainability*, *known*, or *duration* were statistically significant predictors of voting in the model for those who had role models.

Political role models, however, appear to impact other types of political engagement. I look beyond voting at how having a political role model is associated with political participation. For this, I use measures of political participation utilized by the American National Elections Studies, which ask if a respondent has or has not participated in each of the following in the previous twelve months:

- Gone to a political speech, march, rally, or demonstration
- Phoned, emailed, written to, or visited a government official to express your views on a public issue
- Worn a campaign button, put a campaign sticker on your car, or placed a sign in your window or in front of your house
- Given money to any candidate running for public office, any political party, or any other group that supported or opposed candidates

I combine these four questions to form a 4-point scale,[6] where 0 would mean participating in none of these activities and 4 would mean participating in all four of them. As one might guess, people who do all four are pretty rare. In fact, note that the mean value for the entire sample was a meager .88, or, on average, less than a single activity in the previous year. However, the difference between respondents who reported having a role model (μ = 1.31) and those who did not (μ = .43) is dramatically different. Those with a role model were more than three times more active than those that had no role model ($p < .001$). In this instance, these differences do persist in multivariate analysis with numerous controls for factors that have been shown to impact political participation.

As Table 4.1 reveals, a large swath of the variation in political participation in the full sample (Model 1) is accounted for by whether the respondent reported having a role model or not (β = .237, $p < .001$). Models 2 and 3 only account for the variation in the subsample with role models. In Model 2, I add the role model *attainability* variable, which has a signifi-

	Model 1 (full sample)	Model 2 (role model only)	Model 3 (role model only)
TABLE 4.1 IMPACT OF POLITICAL ROLE MODEL AND ROLE MODEL RELATIONSHIP ON POLITICAL PARTICIPATION			
Role model (Y/N)	.237*** (.062)	–	–
Role model attainability	–	.159*** (.015)	.085* (.015)
Role model closeness	–	–	.212*** (.042)
Role model duration	–	−.020 (.067)	−.045 (.069)
Political interest	.265*** (.029)	.238*** (.048)	.236*** (.049)
Age	−.157*** (.002)	−.162** (.003)	−.161*** (.003)
Education	.072** (.016)	.078* (.024)	.053 (.024)
Gender	−.049* (.059)	−.061 (.090)	−.057 (.092)
Race	−.022 (.077)	.017 (.111)	.008 (.112)
Party	.079** (.060)	.120*** (.094)	.124*** (.095)
Observations	1418	772	726
R^2	.243	.184	.223

Note: The outcome variable is the number of political activities reported in the last 12 months. The variable ranges from 0 to 4, and I estimated each model using OLS models. Standard errors in parentheses. $^*p < .05$, $^{**}p < .01$, $^{***}p < .001$.

cant positive impact ($\beta = .159$, $p < .001$) on the political participation of those with role models. This reveals the relationship disputed elsewhere in social psychology: rather than make behavior seem out of reach, a successful role model is more likely to inspire modeled behavior than one whose success seems less attainable. This would be more consistent with ICT, which emphasizes the power of a self-identified role model, rather than one someone may be exposed to but not really associate with in the true sense of role modeling.

In Model 3, I add role model *known* to the model, which also shows a significant positive impact ($\beta = .212$, $p < .001$) on political participation while reducing the coefficient of *attainability* only partially ($\beta = .085$, $p < .05$). Here, the effect of role model closeness is as found elsewhere in role model research; the closer people feel to their role model, the more likely they are to emulate modeled behavior. In this instance, whether by having a personal relationship with their role model or having connected with them on some less personal level, those who had role models who were well known to them were more likely to have higher levels of political participation.

As expected, in neither Model 2 or 3 is the coefficient for role model *duration* sizable or statistically significant. Whether a role model is long standing, recent, or somewhere in between does not appear to be associated with increased or decreased political participation.

Role Models Inspiring Political Attitudes

Americans with and without political role models do not just behave in different ways politically, they believe different things about the U.S. political system. Any political system, especially a democratic one, depends on the faith and confidence of its citizenry. This includes, but is not limited to, political beliefs like whether people feel fairly represented, trust the government to do the right things, or believe they are empowered within the system to affect political change. It also means that attitudes that normalize violence toward political outgroups or in opposition to the government can be dangerous for democratic institutions and society.

I find having a political role model is associated with some normatively good political attitudes but also some troubling ones. First, I create a measure of *perception of representation* from responses about whether individuals feel like they are represented by people like themselves at the local, state, and national levels, creating a scale variable[7] where 0 means they feel their identity ("people like me") is underrepresented at all levels of government and 6 means they feel their identity is overrepresented at all levels ($\mu = 2.2$). As Figure 4.1 shows, those who identify with a political role model feel more represented ($\mu = 2.6$ vs. $\mu = 1.8$, $p < .001$).

Figure 4.1 also demonstrates that the same is true for *political trust*[8] in the federal government, where those with political role models had more than twice as much trust in government ($\mu = .63$) than those without role models ($\mu = .30$, $p < .001$). It should be noted that neither of these values approach even the midpoint (1) of the scale, so aggregate levels of trust in the sample were generally quite low regardless of role model status.

Finally, these differences also are revealed in levels of *political efficacy*,[9] which was asked on a 5-point scale (scale 0–4, $\mu = 1.78$). While here again levels were relatively low among respondents, those with political role

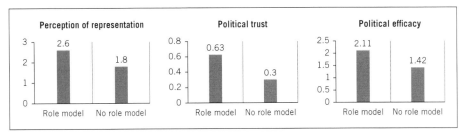

Figure 4.1 Mean Value of Political Attitudes, by Political Role Model Orientation (*Note:* All differences between role model and non–role model identifiers are significant $p < .001$.)

models were substantially more efficacious (μ = 2.11) than those without them (μ = 1.42, p < .001).

These bivariate relationships persist in multivariate analysis and are, in some cases, strengthened for those with role models depending on how attainable and/or well known those role models are to the aspirant (see Tables A.1–A.3 in the appendix). The notable exception to this is that other factors (i.e., political participation) seem to drive the positive inflation of political trust noted in the bivariate relationship, while the presence of a role model serves to erode trust (see Table A.2 in the appendix). These findings are largely consistent with ICT and suggest that the promoting, encouraging, and existence of political role models in American society is a way to promote normatively healthy democratic attitudes toward the government.

Unfortunately, we live in turbulent times for American democracy, and not all the associations between political role models and aspirant attitudes are positive ones. As Figure 4.2 indicates, on two measures of political incivility, *political aggression*[10] and *political violence*[11] (Kalmoe and Mason 2022), the presence of a political role model is associated with less positive attitudes. While the mean value of those reporting a propensity for political aggression was still quite low (μ = .91), those without political role models report dramatically fewer incidents of insulting, threatening, or physically harming people "because of their politics" (μ = .53 vs. μ = 1.26, p < .001). Overall, the likelihood of supporting political violence (μ = 1.33) is also relatively low, but those with political role models were more likely to agree that the country might only be saved by violence (μ = 1.5 vs. μ = 1.15, p < .001).

These same relationships exist in multivariate analysis, as well (see Appendix tables). As ICT predicts, longer, enduring connections to a po-

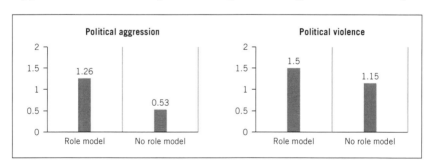

Figure 4.2 Mean Value of Political Aggression and Violence, by Political Role Model Orientation
(*Note:* All differences between role model and non–role model identifiers are significant p < .001.)

litical role model (*duration*) seem to reduce these negative attitudes. Practically speaking, these findings mean that if you have a political role model, you are in good company; about half of Americans do. And that half is likely to be more politically active than those who do not. Furthermore, with a role model, you are more likely to feel good about the government while also being at least a bit scrappy about protecting your view of how it should be. Next, I discuss which individuals Americans identify as political role models, which offers some insight into the influences on political behavior and attitudes revealed thus far.

Who Are These Role Models?

Who are the people modeling this behavior for the American citizenry? Research into role models typically is conducted with the researchers deciding who serves as role models. I let Americans tell me. Not surprisingly, they tend to be high-profile figures who are dominant in the contemporary political landscape, though there is some variation. U.S. presidents are, by far, the most common response. Figure 4.3 illustrates the most frequently mentioned political role models identified by this population.

More than a third of respondents (38.5 percent) named one of the last three U.S. presidents, Joe Biden (13.1 percent), Donald Trump (16.7 percent), and Barack Obama (9 percent), and the two most recent vice presi-

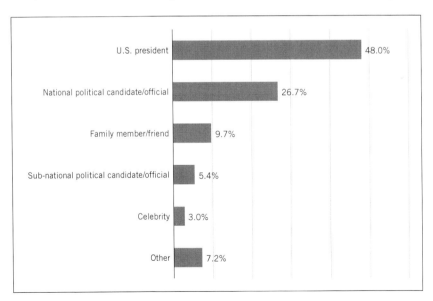

Figure 4.3 Political Role Models, by Category
(*Note:* Graph does not equal 100 percent due to rounding.)

dents, Kamala Harris (6 percent) and Mike Pence (0.5 percent), were also named. Among other national political figures were a number of members of Congress, including Senator Bernie Sanders (D-VT, 2.6 percent), Representative Alexandria Ocasio-Cortez (D-NY, 2.3 percent), and Speaker of the House Nancy Pelosi (D-CA, 0.6 percent). Former first ladies, including former secretary of state and presidential candidate Hillary Clinton (0.9 percent) and Michelle Obama (0.9 percent), were named as well. Respondents pointed to their grandparents, mothers, fathers, children, and politically active friends, and even celebrities like Beyoncé, The Rock, LeBron James, and Kid Rock received mentions. Activists like Stacey Abrams and Martin Luther King Jr. were occasionally mentioned, as were media personalities like Rush Limbaugh and Rachel Maddow.

ICT obviously implies that role models must be inspiring, so I would expect to see these named role models associated with inspiring attributes. I used the most commonly cited traits used to describe political leaders in my previous work (Sweet-Cushman 2021) to reveal what it was about each of these individuals that respondents found appealing about them as role models. Top among these traits were "leader," "confident," "well spoken," "hard working," and "good with people," pointing to the importance of positive, bold, and charismatic figures as potential role models. Negative traits like "power hungry," "controlling," and "manipulative," frequently attributed to elected officials, were significantly unpopular traits for role models. It appears elected officials and other political figures must thread the needle on stereotypes about politicians in order to serve as role models.

With Americans looking to these inspiring figures as political role models, they are positioned to have the kind of influence previously described. I find that certain role models, in particular, have pronounced effects on political behavior and attitudes. For example, in the previous analyses, I find that those with a political role model were more likely to report political aggression and support for political violence (see Figure 4.3). Since 29.5 percent of respondents who identified a political role model identified either President Joe Biden or former president Donald Trump as their role model, I can isolate the impact these controversial figures in American politics have on people who admire them. While it is not true for the other outcomes I test, as Table 4.2 reveals (looking only at those with role models), support for *political violence* is not only encouraged by having a role model and some of their attributes but is also magnified by who that role model is. In this model, those who named Trump as their role model were more likely to be supportive of political violence ($ß = .102, p < .05$). The same is potentially also true for those who name Biden as their role model ($ß = .076, p = .53$), but this result just barely misses conventional measures of

TABLE 4.2 IMPACT OF BIDEN AND TRUMP AS ROLE MODELS ON SUPPORT FOR POLITICAL VIOLENCE

	Role models (only sample)
Biden role model	.076† (.169)
Trump role model	.102* (.157)
Role model attainability	.118** (.018)
Role model closeness	.135*** (.052)
Role model duration	−.125** (.083)
Political interest	−.024 (.058)
Political participation	.121** (.044)
Age	−.167*** (.004)
Education	−.061 (.029)
Gender	−.138*** (.107)
Race	.033 (.134)
Party	.173*** (.126)
Observations	631
R^2	.230

Note: The outcome variable is political violence, and I estimated the model using OLS models. Standard errors in parentheses. $†p < .10$, $*p < .05$, $**p < .01$, $***p < .001$.

statistical significance. It should be noted, too, that I control for political party (which is serving to depress acceptance of violence) in this model, so this is a separate impact of identifying this way with the de facto party leaders. No other single role model appears with enough frequency to investigate whether others might encourage this phenomenon, but that the two most often cited role models do should be a matter of concern.

Ingroup versus Outgroup Role Models

Of course, it is largely Republicans identifying with former president Trump (84.4 percent of those who identified him as their role model) and largely Democrats identifying with President Biden (89 percent of those who identified him as their role model). People are identifying with copartisans. But I find other patterns within various intersections of gender, race, and political party that speak to the stereotype inoculation aspect of ICT: role models in politics can be more important to those who have been historically marginalized in American politics. This is most true if they identify with an ingroup role model—someone who belongs to the same identity group as they do rather than a member of an outgroup with whom their identity differs. First, I explore characteristic differences in who identifies with political role models and whether people choose role models with whom they share an identity. I then turn to how both ingroup and outgroup role models impact the political behavior and attitudes of women versus men[12] and their racial and partisan intersections.

The first thing to note about political role models and identity is that not everyone is equally as likely to identify with a role model. Figure 4.4 reveals the percentage of respondents who identified one or more political role models. Fewer than half of women (49 percent), Republicans (47.4 percent), and Republican women (44.2 percent) reported identifying with a political role model, compared to more than 60 percent of Democratic men (66.4 percent), BIPOC (Black, indigenous, people of color) (63.2 percent), Democrats (62.3 percent), and BIPOC women (61.1 percent). While it is possible this pattern is an artifact of the current U.S. president and vice president (a Democratic man and a BIPOC Democratic woman) as named role models, 84 percent of respondents reported that their identified role model had been their role model for more than a year, and more than 40 percent said their role model had been an influence for more than five years. Regardless, the visibility of some groups in U.S. politics (e.g., BIPOC women) relative to the visibility of others (Republican women) could be reasonably expected to influence whether Americans in these groups feel a role model connection.

And I do find evidence that a majority of people look to someone with whom they share at least one identity. Of those who named role models,

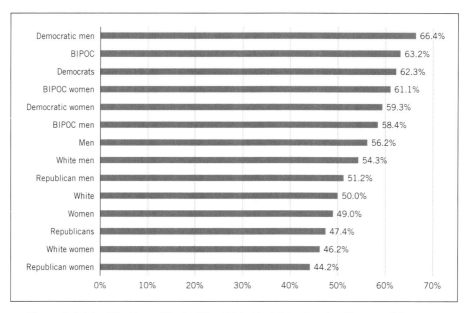

Figure 4.4 Identification with a Political Role Model, by Gender, Race, and Party

61.3 percent named someone from their gender ingroup and 67.2 percent named someone from their racial ingroup. In other words, there was a tendency for men to identify with men, women to identify with women, people who are white to identify with those who are also white, and BIPOC respondents to identify with BIPOC role models.

ICT posits that this ingroup identification will not matter as much for those whose presence in American politics has been historically unquestioned. White men or male partisans have always been included in political processes, whereas female and BIPOC citizens have not and in many ways continue to be marginalized in the political arena. For these women, and maybe especially BIPOC and Republican ones, the existence of an ingroup role model serves to "inoculate" against the negative impact of marginalization and underrepresentation.

Everyone tends to choose a copartisan, so I do not analyze the impact of partisan intersections other than to note the differences in Figure 4.4 where Democrats are more likely to have political role models than are Republicans. However, role model identification along gender and racial identities varies.

Unfortunately, the sample sizes get too small among those with role models to meaningfully look at how all the interactions for race and gender impact political behavior and political attitudes. However, there are main effects of having a political role model who is of the same gender and racial ingroup for *voting* ($p < .05$), *political participation* ($p < .05$), *perception of representation* ($p < .05$), *political aggression* ($p < .001$), and *political violence* ($p < .05$). In other words, individuals who identify with a role model who shares their gender and race are more likely to vote, be politically active, and feel they are appropriately represented at all levels of government. Figure 4.5 displays the variation in these by gender and racial group for those who identify ingroup versus outgroup role models. They are also more likely to report participating in acts of political aggression and being supportive of political violence, which is displayed for each gender and racial group by in- and outgroup role models (as seen in Figure 4.6, following).

Figure 4.5 illustrates some scenarios where the "inoculation" effect in ICT is perhaps at play. While the smaller subsample sizes do not allow for definitive generalization, the enhanced likelihood of voting for BIPOC women with BIPOC women role models and of political participation by BIPOC men with BIPOC men role models is suggestive that there may be an impact on someone's political behavior when their role models share their identity.

It seems as though, rather than offering historically marginalized Americans a rosier perception of representation, it makes them more aware that

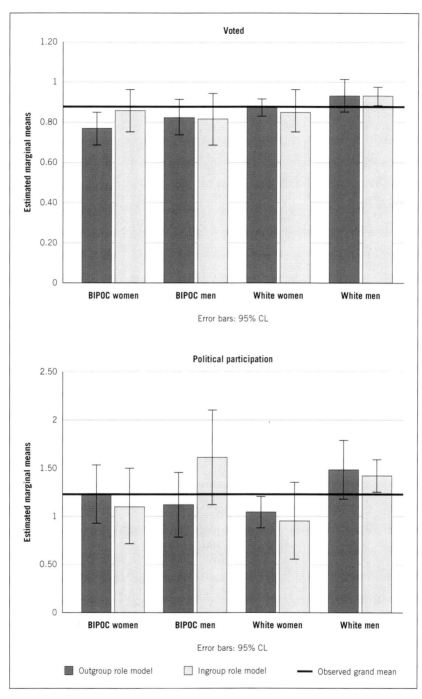

Figure 4.5 Mean Differences in Political Behavior by Identity Group and In-/Outgroup Political Role Models

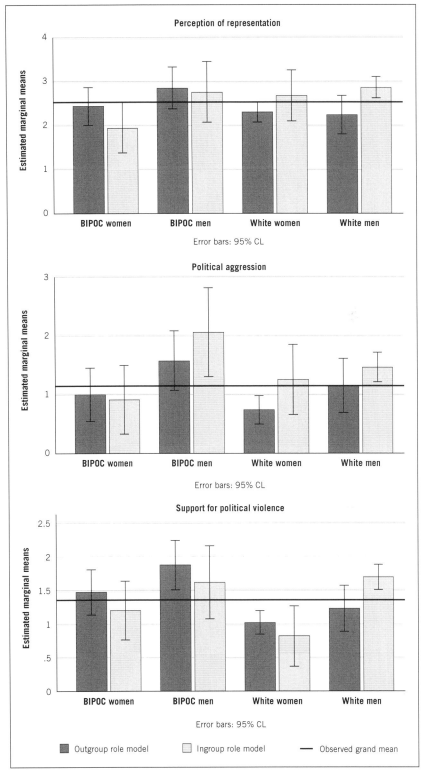

Figure 4.6 Mean Differences in Political Attitudes by Identity Group and In-/Outgroup Political Role Models

they remain unrepresented. Though white women with an ingroup role model view politics as more equally representing them, BIPOC (and especially BIPOC women) are more likely to view politics as less representative of their identity (see Figure 4.6), which is actually an accurate perception of U.S. politics on aggregate. On one hand, while recognizing the reality of the political environment is good, feeling unrepresented likely is not.

Figure 4.6 also reveals an interesting contradiction in the impact of ingroup political role models on more aggressive attitudes in American politics. Sample size again makes it difficult to say more definitively, but the patterns appear to be that—across the board—ingroup role models are associated with higher levels of political aggression but reduce support for violence among everyone but the historically dominant group within American politics, white men. It is possible this difference reflects a reality in American politics where marginalized citizens feel threatened in their political environments and are responding to that reality while remaining reluctant to escalate into violence. Tracking these attitudes over time and as partisan control of government changes would offer additional insights.

Political Role Models in Action: Inspiring Engaged Citizenship

Remember my role model city councilperson, Erika Strassburger? She did not have a primary opponent as she sought reelection in 2021. Normally that would mean volunteers and donors would invest elsewhere or perhaps not be as active in local politics as they might be if their candidate was facing a challenge. However, Councilperson Strassburger was out canvassing voters and fundraising for purposes other than fending off an opponent, and I joined her because I felt inspired by her presence in local government.

Now, as a political scientist, I am certainly not normal in any number of ways, but my response to a political role model might be. What I have revealed in this chapter is that there are positive implications for political behavior (e.g., increased political participation) and political attitudes (e.g., increased political efficacy) for those who have political role models, especially ones they feel close to. On the other hand, the deeper connection to American politics that a political role model helps facilitate has a downside in the contemporary political environment. My data also shows that individuals with political role models have a greater sense that they need to defend their view of politics by being more aggressive in how they oppose those who threaten it or even supporting violence to "safeguard" the government.

There is some limited evidence, too, that both this good effect and the more troubling one are further encouraged when someone's political role model shares their identity, such as Councilperson Strassburger and I. This offers some protection against feeling marginalized in a way that suppresses political engagement for those who have been historically left out of politics. But this connection may also shorten the fuse leading to more aggressive political acts. This area of research admittedly needs more focused investigation and would benefit from both experimental evidence that isolates the causal mechanism and more qualitative research that seeks to understand what about role models inspires both deeper and more protective engagement. I scratch the surface of the former in Chapter 6.

Overall, however, ICT offers insight into how everyday Americans interact with their political environment. About half of people can identify a political role model, and the half that do are decidedly more engaged but also more likely to support violence. Those who do have political role models, and especially those who have historically not been well integrated into American politics, can also benefit from seeing and admiring someone who shares their gender or (and especially) racial identity. These findings offer promising potential for how U.S. presidents, other national elected officials, state and local officials, and even family members can encourage political engagement and think deeply about how they can discourage political aggression.

In Chapter 5, I turn to looking at how these political elites—using candidates for political office—also respond to role models in their own political behavior and how role models are associated with various political attitudes. This is arguably the pipeline not just to political leadership but also to political role modeling, so these insights have profound implications.

5

Political Role Models and Candidate Jane

In 2021, the Black educator, suffragist, and civil rights activist Mary McLeod Bethune was enshrined in the U.S. Capitol—replacing a confederate general—to represent Florida in the National Statuary Hall. More than 60 years after her death, Bethune continues to inspire Black women. Val Demings (D-FL), former U.S. representative and candidate for U.S. Senate, for example, has touted her late role model's activism as essential to her own career. She stated, "Mary McLeod Bethune was the most powerful woman I can remember as a child. She has been an inspiration throughout my whole life" (Jones 2020). Role models have the potential to inspire Americans who take what is arguably the deepest plunge into U.S. civic life: running for office.

Running for office is not actually a very common thing in terms of political participation (Verba, Schlozman, and Brady 1995), which has been a challenge in studying who runs and, especially, who does not (Sweet-Cushman 2014). Noting what little we know about those who do run for office, in 2014 the Pew Research Center (Motel 2014) first asked a representative sample of Americans if they had ever sought elective office. About 2 percent indicated they had. This small fraction of Americans reflects well-documented discrepancies between the general population and those who represent us (Ashe and Stewart 2012; Czudnowski 1975; Katz 2001; Mansbridge 1999; Schwartz 1969) along lines of gender (Childs and Hughes 2018; Matland 2005), race (Barnes 2016; Malhotra and Raso 2007), socioeconomic status (Carnes 2012; Giger, Rosset, and Bernauer 2012), and other demographics. Pew found that those who have run for office are more likely to be white, male, and educated (Motel 2014).

This same Pew study also found that this group was more likely to participate in politics in other ways, noting that 35 percent of those that had previously run for office had also donated to other political candidates and causes (Motel 2014). People who run for office are relatively rare in the United States, but they represent a disproportionate percentage of people who dominate political activities of many kinds.

In many ways candidates for political office are inspired to run by similar motives. In Deckman's study of candidates for school board—where candidates are typically getting their political feet wet—most candidates were motivated by similar professional, policy, and community goals. Men were somewhat more likely to be motivated by a desire to apply their value system to education policymaking (Deckman 2007). Communal goals are also more motivating (than power-related ones) to women considering a candidacy (Schneider et al. 2016). Communities, in general, are of utmost importance for women's political aspirations. Women need members of their families, political networks, religious institutions, and so forth to provide support and encouragement (Crowder-Meyer 2020; Sweet-Cushman 2018b) for their political aspirations more than men do, and these are potential sources of political role models.

While the study of women's political ambition has offered a great deal of insight into why women run for office at rates much lower than men, far less is known about how other identities may encourage political candidates. As Shames (2017) argues, intersectional analysis of political ambition poses a multitude of challenges, and capturing all aspects of identity is impractical anyway. Nonetheless, certainly more needs to be known about the motivations of those who are underrepresented in candidacies for political office.

Beyond just being more likely to be white, male, and educated, political candidates are also much more likely to emerge from certain professions. A majority of the country's elected officials have backgrounds in law, business, education, or advocacy (Lawless and Fox 2005, 2010). Furthermore, as Lawless and Fox (2005) revealed when they surveyed men and women with these backgrounds, those with a politicized upbringing were nearly twice as likely to consider running for office than those that did not grow up in environments where politics were salient. Consider the words of former president George W. Bush as he eulogized his father, former president George H. W. Bush:

Dad taught us that public service is noble and necessary; that one can serve with integrity and hold true to the important values, like faith and family. He strongly believed that it was important to give back to the community and country in which one lived. . . . Of course, Dad taught me another special lesson. He showed me what it means to be a president who serves with integrity, leads with courage, and acts with love in his heart for the citizens of our country. (Bush 2018)

There can be no doubt that the 43rd president's path to the White House was enormously influenced by a political role model in his life, his father, who was the 41st president of the United States. Bush's words upon his father's death clearly recognize the modeling he received growing up in a politicized home. And it is easy to find examples of other families where the family business is politics, with parents seemingly passing down a penchant for public service to their children. Since men are 22 percent more likely to report having had a politicized upbringing (Lawless and Fox 2005), it is no surprise that they are also significantly more likely to run for office.

Socialization would absolutely suggest that politically active parents are more likely to foster future political candidates (Beck and Jennings 1982; Lawless and Fox 2005), but this also seems to be only one piece of the puzzle. In this chapter, I again use ICT as a guide in exploring how role models inspire political elites to run for elective office. This examination focuses on three primary queries. First, *who serves as political role models for people who run for office?*

The other two questions tie directly to my theoretical predictions. As we saw in Chapter 4, I affirmed the *Inspired Citizenship Motivation Prediction*'s assertion that individuals with deep connections to a role model are more likely to hold positive political attitudes and participate more in politics. Since the most intense commitment and the strongest motivation to participate in the political system involve putting oneself forth as a political candidate, it would seem likely that role models are even more essential in fostering candidate emergence. *Do some types of role models inspire more successful candidates?*

And finally, ICT would also contend, as I suggest in the *Inspired Citizenship Inoculation Prediction*, that there would be particular value in political role models for candidates for office who have historically marginalized identities. *Do these candidates tend to identify with ingroup role models? Are those who do more or less successful as candidates?*

Data and Methods

To address these questions, I again use an original survey, this time of candidates for elective office across the country who ran during the general or primary elections in 2020. This survey was fielded immediately following the November general election in order to reach candidates before campaign emails expired or became unattended and while their motivations for running for office might still be fresh. The survey was distributed to a list of candidates for statewide and federal offices in all U.S. states and territories maintained by the marketing firm KnowWho using QualtricsXM survey software. The complete list was composed of 12,776 identified and unique candidate emails, of which 1,229 bounced—most of which were primary candidate campaigns that, by November, were no longer maintaining their campaign email addresses. The initial invitation to participate was sent on November 11, 2020, with one follow-up serving as a reminder one week later. The survey was closed on December 13, 2020. The resultant sample ($n = 11,547$) yielded 1,561 completed survey responses, a 13.5 percent response rate.

Elite response rates tend to be very low, and this was to be expected especially given that these were campaign contacts that were initiated after the campaign had concluded and I could not truly verify how many of the email addresses were still valid. It is also not inconsistent with surveys of other elite samples (Farris and Holman 2017; Holman 2014; Maestas, Neely, and Richardson 2003; Sweet-Cushman 2018b).

There was nonetheless good variation in those who responded. A little more than a quarter (27.4 percent) won their races, an overrepresentation of "winners," and 16.6 percent were incumbents—perhaps an indication that more serious candidates were more likely respond. Race, gender, and party information was maintained by KnowWho and not collected directly from the respondents. Race information was only available for just over one-third (37.2 percent) of the respondents, and of those, 7.4 percent were non-white, which resulted in an under sampling of marginalized identities and made it, like in Chapter 4, statistically challenging to analyze identity subsamples. Women were somewhat more represented in the sample, as 39.2 percent of the respondents were women. More Democrats (49.8 percent) than Republicans (36.7 percent) were represented, but there was also representation from 13 minor parties, too.

Do Candidates for Political Office Identify with Role Models?

The most basic premise of ICT is that people tend to look up to people they know or know of as models of political behavior. As we saw in Chapter 4, those who had political role models were more likely to be politically active, feel more represented in government, and have greater political trust and efficacy. In this chapter, I look at what inspires people who run for elective office. This is always—at least symbolically—a significant political commitment and frequently requires much energy, time, and resources from candidates and their families to run, let alone serve if elected. As such, it is easy to image that for these Americans, there is an even stronger association between role models and their political participation.

Findings

Do Political Role Models Encourage
Candidate Emergence?

Unfortunately, finding a comparison group of people who considered a candidacy but ultimately did not run is difficult, so I cannot isolate the relationship between political role models and candidate emergence, but I am able to look at how those who do run differ from the general population (Chapter 4), whether political role models are more common among those who win their races, who their role models are and what traits they most admire, whether they are interested in running again, and how having role models impacts candidate motivation for running and political career goals. ICT would anticipate that political role models would connect most with viable candidates and have a normatively positive impact on the motivation for and goals of their candidacy. These positive associations should be magnified for those with ingroup role models and especially for candidates who have been historically underrepresented in politics—women and BIPOC candidates.

Before asking these candidates for political office to consider and identify their role models, I assess whether they have a sense for the presence of political role models in their lives generally. I use a battery of 15 questions for this adapted from the Influence of Others on Academic Career Decisions Scale (IOACDS) to create an Influence of Others on Political Decisions and Careers Scale (IOPDCS). The IOACDS scale was originally designed to help investigate a host of unanswered questions about the impact of role models on aspirants' career choices:

> These questions remain, in part, because of a lack of instruments designed to measure various role model influences on academic and career decisions. This research was designed to develop a measure of role model influence that may help test theories regarding the nature and influence of role models. (Nauta and Kokaly 2001, 81)

The IOPDCS adapted version in the following list[1] capitalizes on the validity and reliability of the IOACDS to measure the degree to which candidates recognize a political role model or models as resources to their political careers. I refined the items in the scale to reflect the nature of political
role models, creating more specificity in the types of individuals the scale
asks respondents to identify so as to associate them with politics, political
careers, and political environments:

1. There is someone I can count on to be there if I need support
   when I make choices about my political career.
2. There is someone who helps me weight the pros and cons of political choices I make.
3. There is someone who helps me consider options for my political career.
4. There is no one who shows me how to get where I am going with
   my political career. (R)
5. There is someone who supports me in the choices I make for
   my political career.
6. There is someone who stands by me when I make important
   political decisions.
7. There is no one who supports me when I make decisions about
   my political career. (R)
8. There is someone who tells or shows me general strategies for
   a successful political career.
9. There is someone I am trying to be like in my political pursuits.
10. There is no one particularly inspirational to me in the political
    path I am pursuing. (R)
11. In the political path I am pursuing, there is someone I admire.
12. There is no one I am trying to be like in my political pursuits. (R)
13. I have a political mentor.
14. I know of someone who has a political career like the one I'd
    like to have.
15. In the political path I am pursuing, there is no one who inspires
    me. (R)

I combined these items[2] to form a composite score for each respondent, with higher scores indicating a stronger presence of political role models in someone's life. On a 7-point scale, scores ranged from a minimum
of 0 (respondent strongly disagreed with all the statements on the scale)
to 90 (respondent strongly agreed with all the statements on the scale).

The mean composite score was 60, indicating that there was a relatively strong sense of having political role models within this sample. White women, in particular, were above the mean with an average score of 63.7. The IOPDCS scores by race and gender are reflected in Figure 5.1. Differences were statistically significant by gender ($p < .001$) and remain significant when split by party, meaning Democratic (63.7) and Republican women (61.4) had stronger senses of having political role models than their male counterparts ($p < .001$). Results did not vary statistically by race ($p = .190$). Understandably, those who identified with a third or independent political party appeared to have the least connection with political role models (55.1).

This sense of having a political role model that respondents of all types reported is also reflected in a more direct question that asked these candidates for political office—like in Chapter 4—if there was anyone they identified as a political role model.[3] More than eight out of ten (81.8 percent) respondents agreed that they did have someone they identified with this way, though not all subsequently identified this person by name. Across all identity groups (gender, race, party, and gender by race and party), it was vastly more likely that individuals reported having a role model than not. The percent of those who identified with political role models, however, was statistically different within identity groups ($p < .05$). As opposed to the general population examined in Chapter 4, where white women were the least likely to identify with political role models, among this elite sam-

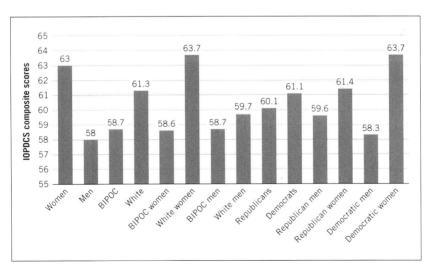

Figure 5.1 Mean Values of IOPDCS, by Gender, Race, and Political Party Affiliation

ple, they were the most likely to identify with a role model (89.9 percent), with BIPOC men (87.5 percent), BIPOC women (83.8 percent), and white men (82 percent) each reporting role models at a slightly lower rate.

Those who have political role models do not appear to be motivated to run by inherently different things than those who do. There are no statistically significant differences between the two groups of candidates on any of the motivations to run I queried them about. Approximately equal percentages of both groups said they were motivated to run for office by the same things. For example, the most important reason for their candidacies, for both those with role models ($\mu = 1.97$) and those without ($\mu = 1.94$), was "a chance to make the community a better place to live." Similarly, the least motivating factor for both those with role models ($\mu = .45$) and those without ($\mu = .39$) was "a chance to further my job and/or professional goals."[4]

Where these two groups do differ is in whether they felt like they belonged in politics. "Belongingness" is a measure of social connectedness and assurance that reveals how accepted in a social space a person feels (Lee and Robbins 1995). Adapted from measures of belongingness in psychology, respondents were asked how strongly they agreed that they belonged in politics, as well as whether they felt like an outsider, disconnected, or rejected in politics. I combined these four measures to form a 16-point belongingness index ($\mu = 10.76$), where the higher the number on the scale, the more a respondent feels a sense of belonging in politics. ICT would suggest that those with role models in politics are less likely to feel like they do not belong in politics because having a role model connects them to the political domain. However, it might also predict that those who feel less like they belong are more likely to seek out and connect with role models to compensate for the sense of inadequacy. Indeed, the former appears to be true, as those without role models express more disconnect than those who do have role models ($\mu = 11.04$ vs. $\mu = 9.42$, $p < .001$).

Who Are the Role Models?

In contrast to the general population sample, in which nearly half (48 percent) of respondents reported their political role model was a U.S. president (current or former), candidates for elective office report a more diverse selection of role models. The two most common responses from the general population, former president Donald Trump (3.2 percent) and current president Joe Biden (< 1 percent), factor only minimally into these reports from 2020 political candidates. Instead, these candidates predominantly report that various other national or state-level political figures have

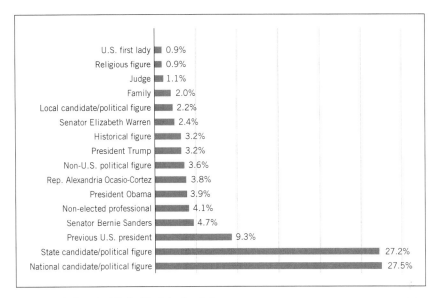

Figure 5.2 Political Role Models, by Category

been a source of inspiration for them (Figure 5.2). They were also more likely to name contemporary high-profile political figures like Representative Alexandria Ocasio-Cortez (D-NY) and Senator Bernie Sanders (I-VT).

The difference between this sample of political candidates and the general population sample could not be starker. Recall in Chapter 4 that only about half of that sample (52.1 percent) had a political role model, so it can really be said that people who run for office are much more likely to identify with a role model than those who sit more on the sidelines of electoral politics. These candidates also tend to have a different orientation to their role models than do those in the general public. While they report having had their role model for the same *duration* as those in the general sample, they report that their role models are much more well *known* ($\mu = 1.71$ vs. $\mu = .971$, $p < .001$) to them and that their role models' successes are less *attainable* ($\mu = 7.91$ vs. $\mu = 8.3$, $p < .05$), though this lower evaluation among political candidates is driven by those who lost their races. Those who won their races rated their political role models as similarly attainable to the general population sample.

While candidates for office seem to identify with very different role models than the general population, they do report valuing similar traits in those role models (and eschewing negative ones). Like I find in Chapter 4 in the general population, political candidates also most value a role model as a "leader," and significant majorities appear to recognize the importance of a charismatic and bold figure. Perhaps because these political candidates are more likely to recognize more acutely some of the traits the political sphere requires, they were somewhat more likely to value confident, influential, motivated, and successful role models. These would seem to be valuable traits for aspirants who want to be successful in electoral politics to emulate.

Is a Role Model a Winning Strategy?

Survey data makes it difficult to evaluate whether having a political role model makes people more likely to win or whether winners are more likely to have political role models—or perhaps both. In general, the impact of role models on political candidates appears somewhat less clear in the context of political candidates than in the general population, but this is to be expected. Recall in Chapter 3 that psychology has wrestled with the limitations of role models when their success is perceived as achievable. Given that political candidates very clearly aspire to achievements that their political role models have reached, it is quite possible that these highly successful role models suppress some of the candidates' own success.

Nonetheless, the *Inspired Citizenship Motivation Prediction* anticipates that a connection to a role model is generally a positive influence on political candidates, potentially related to greater success and persistence as candidates. Only one category (see Figure 5.3) of role model is associated with a subset of more winning candidates than losing, and that is those who identified with judges as role models, though this is an exceptionally small subset ($n = 7$). However, as Figure 5.3 illustrates, there is variation in what percentage were unsuccessful in their 2020 campaigns within the various categories of role models, ranging from the most successful (those with judicial role models, 57.1 percent) to the least (those who named President Obama, 5.9 percent). Many of these categories had too few cases to provide meaningful comparisons of success, but the two largest categories of political role models, national officials/political candidates (18 percent) and state officials/political candidates (35.5 percent), had statistically significant differences in success ($p < .05$).[5]

Turning to the features of the relationship these candidates report having with their role models—or role model orientation—I find that while the bivariate relationship between having a role model and campaign success only reaches marginal significance ($p = .095$), including the orientation to role models (*attainability*, *known*, and *duration*) in multivariate analysis reveals that (see Table A.6 in the appendix), controlling for major party status and incumbency, believing that the success of a political role model is achievable is actually associated with a slightly decreased likelihood

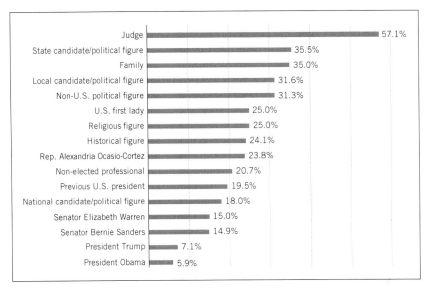

Figure 5.3 Percentage of Candidates Who Won Their Races, by Type of Role Model

of candidates winning their race (ß = .868, $p < .10$), suggesting that perhaps political candidates tend to be a bit more ambitious than is realistic. Just because role models may have inspired candidates to run does not mean that inspiration is necessarily part of a rational candidacy or one launched with winning as the expected outcome. The proximity (*known*) to a role model and the length of that connection (*duration*) do not reveal an effect. Men with role models were also more than twice as likely to win than were women with role models, though also only at the level of marginal significance (ß = 2.009, $p < .10$).

For candidates who lost their 2020 bid, those with role models were somewhat more likely to express an interest in running for office again in the future ($\mu = 2.20$ vs. $\mu = 2.02$)[6] ($p < .05$). For these candidates with political role models, the attainability of their role model's success (*attainability*) and their closeness (*known*) encourage them to continue to seek political office—though these findings are marginally significant. As Table 5.1 illustrates, length of relationship with one's role model (*duration*) does not encourage a candidate to want to get back on the campaign horse (so to speak) after a loss, but—quite intuitively—believing that their role model's success is achievable does increase their interest in running again, especially when that role model is more well known to the candidate.

Among those with role models, incumbents who lost were more likely to throw in the towel after their loss, as were BIPOC candidates, but wom-

TABLE 5.1 IMPACT OF ROLE MODEL ORIENTATION ON INTEREST IN RUNNING AGAIN	
Role model attainability	.154† (.020)
Role model known	.139† (.050)
Role model duration	.112 (.056)
Incumbency	−.212* (.267)
Major party	−.243 (.087)
Gender	.150† (.120)
Race	−.138† (.147)
Observations	559
R^2	.143

Note: The outcome variable is how interested in running for office in the future. The variable is coded 0 = never and 3 = definitely, and I estimated each model using OLS regression. Coefficient; standard errors in parentheses. †$p < .10$, *$p < .05$.

en were somewhat more resilient; both gender and race are marginally significant. I now turn to exploring the potential stereotype inoculation effects on political candidacies that may be associated with having a political role model with whom the candidate shares features of their identity.

Are Ingroup Political Role Models More Effective?

If you are a Native American woman running for office in the United States, you are pretty rare. Only three Native American women have ever served in the U.S. Congress, and the first were only elected in 2018. That does not bode well for descriptive representation for women of native heritage, and it likely means that identifying a role model—for politically up-and-coming Native American women—is more challenging. That is the entire premise behind a campaign training specifically for indigenous women sponsored by Native Action Network, a nonprofit out of Seattle. The "boot camp" features lots of nuts and bolts of running for office that any candidate for office would need, of course, but it also cultivates vertical and horizontal relationship building among and between indigenous women considering a run for office. The women who participate are relieved to find women like them engaging in politics in their communities and beyond. As participant Lisa Young of Redmond, Oregon, said:

> [Being] here allowed me to re-energize and say I can be that person of service even though I know there's going to be barriers. . . . I think these women strengthened me a little bit. Enough to say, OK, I'm less afraid today than I was before. (quoted in Gordon 2022)

Campaign trainings, as I discuss more in Chapter 7, often intuitively use role models to inspire people considering a run for political office and tend to present those who can be emulated by aspirants to elective office. For instance, the Native Action Network and plenty of other trainings offer up role models with whom the potential candidates share an identity. ICT would suggest that employing potential role models who share an identity can be even more effective than those who do not. In the following analyses, I examine this aspect of the theory. Do ingroup role models provide an inoculation effect, as the *Inspired Citizenship Inoculation Prediction* asserts?

To test this prediction, I rely on the KnowWho coding of candidates on race and gender. A research assistant coded each candidate's role model according to whether their gender matched or not, their race matched or not, or—in either case—we were unable to determine whether there was a match. Here, gender is a more reliable test than race since the KnowWho data only identifies candidate race for about one-third of the respondents, and of those, not all identify with role models, leaving a much smaller subsample to work with.

Within the subset of candidates who identify with a political role model, 61.3 percent identify with someone who shares their gender and 32.7 percent identify with someone who shares their race. Only 3.5 percent identify a role model from a racial outgroup. Within the sample of those for whom I have identifying information on both gender and race and who have a role model ($n = 287$), 66.9 percent share both identities with their role model. These numbers are driven by white men, 84.3 percent of whom identify with a white male role model. With the relative lack of people of color and women in positions that tend to solicit aspiration from political candidates, it is not surprising that only about half of BIPOC women (54.5 percent) and BIPOC men (54.1 percent) identify with someone who also is not white and shares their gender. Most dramatically, white women were less likely to share both these identities with their political role models, at only 50 percent. As I previously noted, white women in the general population were the least likely to identify with a role model, while they were the most likely among the political candidates. It would appear that difference may exist between the two populations because white women who are candidates more frequently go looking outside their race and gender for role models.

It would also seem, from these percentages, that white men have a plethora of high-profile options with whom to identify, while others (BIPOC men and women and white women) do not. While this results in white women identifying with someone with whom they share only partial identity (47.8 percent) or none at all (2.2 percent), female and male BIPOC candidates appear much more likely (40.9 percent and 37.8 percent, respectively) to recognize the disparity in potential role models and seem more inclined to seek out someone who is not white but shares their gender identity. It is worth noting that while identifying with a fully outgroup role model—someone who shares neither their gender nor their racial identity—was relatively rare for all those who identified a role model, not a single white man identified a BIPOC woman as a role model (0 percent). White women, BIPOC women, and BIPOC men identified a fully outgroup role model 2.2, 4.5, and 8.1 percent of the time, respectively. While it might seem like this likelihood would be tied to how underrepresented these candidates feel or how strong their sense of belonging in the realm of politics might be, neither of these variables have statistically significant effects on whether they identify with someone who shares their identity. Rather, racial and gender identities are predictive of whether someone identifies with an ingroup role model. Party, incumbency, and whether a candidate won also do not seem to make it any more likely for a candidate to have an ingroup role model (see Table A.7 in the appendix). In essence, if there are an abundance of role models who look like you in the political world, as a political candidate, you probably have one. If there are not, you might look to someone with whom you share only a partial identity or, infrequently, look to an outgroup role model. Or maybe, like we saw with white women, you are less likely to have a role model at all.

Arguably more important, however, is how these role model relationships are associated with whether a candidate was successful or is interested in running for office again in the future. The *Inspired Citizenship Inoculation Prediction* posits that a relationship with an ingroup role model will be associated with greater success and persistence in electoral politics. Of course, a vast majority of candidates do lose their races regardless of any other factors, especially among those who ran in the primaries. However, those who have a fully ingroup role model were more than 4 percent more successful (37.7 percent won) than those who have a partial ingroup role model (33 percent) or a fully outgroup role model (33.3 percent), though this difference is only marginally significant ($p < .093$) and does not persist in multivariate analysis where incumbency and major party status are obvious and substantial contributors to campaign success (see Table A.8 in the appendix). Given the complexity of political campaigns and the multitude of factors that contribute to wins and losses (e.g., fundraising, open seats, voter turnout), it is not surprising that I do not find evidence of an impact of something so nuanced.

However, electoral persistence, measured here by interest in running for office again in the future, is not dependent on the whims of the voters but rather the calculations of the prospective candidate. I do find that those with ingroup role models are ever so slightly more interested in running for office again in the future than those with partially ingroup or fully outgroup role models ($\mu = 2.21$ vs. $\mu = 2.18$, 2.14 respectively), though these differences are not at all significant and, again, multivariate analysis reveals no impact of ingroup role models either.

Further analysis continues to reveal that political role models are primarily serving a motivation function for their aspirants, with less evidence of an inoculation effect. On aggregate, there is no statistically significant impact of sharing an identity on the sense of belonging that those with political role models have, and, in fact, sharing a racial identity may have a slightly negative impact (see Table A.9 in the appendix). The lack of inoculation persists when controlling for incumbency, major party status, whether the candidate won or not, and features of the role model relationship.

Nonetheless, the interaction of race and having a racial ingroup role model is relevant ($p < .001$) here despite its apparent contradiction of the theorized inoculation effect. As Figure 5.4 demonstrates, when controlling for whether a candidate won, incumbency, major party status, gender, and race, we can see that white candidates and BIPOC candidates have quite opposite effects of having a racial ingroup member as a role model.[7] For white candidates (men and women), identifying with someone who is also white makes them feel more like they belong in politics, and belonging is depressed by having an outgroup role model. At the same time, a racial outgroup role model for BIPOC candidates (again, men and women) inspires a greater sense of belonging, while a role model from a racial ingroup results in much lower levels of belonging.

There is one way that in-/outgroup role models appear to make a difference in these political candidacies. Recall that I did not find statistically significant differences between the motivations for running for office that candidates report; they are motivated to run by the same things. There are, however, some small differences in what spurred a run for office by those with ingroup versus fully outgroup role models. Most notably, those with outgroup role models indicated that a desire to garner political experience was more important to their candidacies than did those who had ingroup role models ($p < .05$). This may mean that candidates who turn to role models who do not match their identity feel less secure about their qualifications to run. I interpret this ambiguously, however, since other mea-

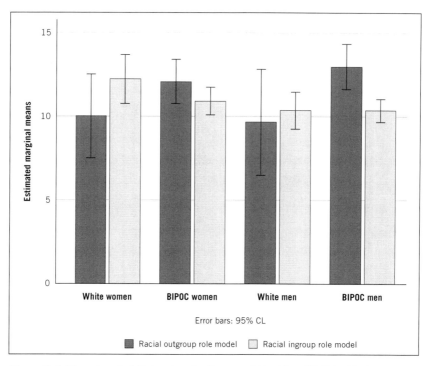

Figure 5.4 Mean Level of Belonging, by Race and Identity of Political Role Model

sures of belonging and perceptions of representation do not seem to overtly corroborate this interpretation. There is, though, some potential for this association with ingroup role models to be viewed as positive for diversifying representation.

Conclusion

In sum, political candidates are much more likely to identify with a role model than is the general public, to the tune of about 30 percent. More respondents in the political candidate sample discussed in this chapter identify with a role model than those in the general population sample discussed in Chapter 4. The IOPDCS scale—which asks respondents about political role models in the abstract—revealed that in this elite sample, women were more likely to have political influences than men. Interestingly, the group in the general population least likely to report a political role model—white women—is the group among political candidates that most frequently reported having a role model. Nearly nine in ten white women candidates have a political role model.

Within the two parties, Democrats were more likely to have role model influences than Republicans, and Democratic and Republican women report more influence than their partisan male counterparts. This pattern is almost the opposite of the pattern in the general population where white women Republicans were the least likely to have found political inspiration. This dramatic difference between white women in the general population and white women in the candidate pool is remarkable and bears further investigation outside the pages of this work.

In all, more than 80 percent of the candidates surveyed identified a specific person in their lives who was a political role model. Like the general population, there is significant support for the idea that political role models have a positive motivating effect on the political behavior of those seeking political office. Political candidates are, however, much more likely than the general population to have role models and to draw them from a more diverse set of potential aspirational figures. Where U.S. presidents (current and former) dominated among respondents in Chapter 4, the political candidates examined in this chapter looked less to the presidency and more to other national or state-level elected officials and, more commonly, to people they personally knew.

In support of the motivation aspect of ICT, I find that those with role models are more likely to feel a sense of belonging in politics, win their races, and be interested in running in the future. However, there is much less support for inoculation effects among political candidates than there was in the general population. Having an ingroup role model who shares your gender or race (or both) does not appear to be associated with much additional benefit to candidates but offers a bit of insight into why they might run in the first place.

Political candidates are basically unicorns in the American public because they are so exceptionally rare. These unique individuals are willing to make a significant commitment to American politics (e.g., running for political office), making it unsurprising that ICT would apply differently to them than it does to those with less significant commitments to the political sphere. However, since they are also more apt to recognize the political inspiration available and to directly identify with political role models, it is also important that candidates have the right types of people and behavior to aspire to.

In Chapter 7, I attempt to fill the hole in the empirical understanding permitted by the survey data I have thus far been relying on to examine the impact of role models on political elites like those examined in this chapter. Through a field experiment with women interested in running for political office, I show where it is possible to make causal claims about the impact of role models and also where causality may be elusive. These findings, and the experimental evidence from a general population sample I discuss next in Chapter 6, will aid in determining whether people (both general public and political candidates) who have political role models are simply quintessentially different than those who do not or if there is something about having a political role model that causes these differences.

6

Political Role Models Gently Shaping
the American Political Landscape?

At this point, I have established that Americans, including political candidates, are more likely than not to say that they have a political role model. These role models tend to be obvious figures in U.S. politics, such as the president, former presidents, or other national political leaders. In some cases, these connections are associated with differences in political behavior or political attitudes; in the case of political candidates, role model effects are connected to their sense of belonging in politics, their resilience as candidates, and their motivations for running for office. While the duration of connection with their professed role model does not seem to matter, in various ways the strength of that connection and the attainability of the modeled behavior do.

Nonetheless, the preceding two chapters leave me (and hopefully you) with some unanswered questions. In this chapter, I address two primary questions that remain. First, *are role models causing these differences, or are people with political role models just different kinds of people? Could there be something just quintessentially different about people who identify with role models that leads them to exhibit these differences?*

The second question is, *if role models have the capacity to shape attitudes and behavior, can they be used in normatively positive ways to improve citizen or candidate orientations to American democracy or even worsen it?* If a political role model encourages participating in a protest, for example, are people more likely to follow that person's lead than those making their participatory choices without a role model's influence.

Barriers to Causation

Both these propositions require causality be established for role model effects. In other words, if we were able to, for example, strip away all the things that create variability in whether someone feels politically efficacious or not or whether a candidate who loses their bid for office wants to run again, would there be an independent effect of the influence of a role model? Would there be a role model effect? This is an important question, but there are significant challenges in determining causality in the relationship between having a political role model and the patterns in political behavior and attitudes described in Chapters 4 and 5. Most importantly, as a researcher, I cannot force someone to have a role model attachment, especially not an enduring one.

Imagine, for example, that you are a political independent who does not feel a connection to one of the two major political parties, which is an increasingly common scenario (Gallup, n.d.). Many of these now 40 percent of Americans imagine themselves above partisan politics, and they eschew party labels and attachments (Klar and Krupnikov 2016). While it has not been tested empirically, it is easy to imagine that even if you consistently vote for one party or the other, as three of four independents do (Klar and Krupnikov 2016), exposure to a presumptive political role model would not inspire attachment, let alone aspirations. In the same vein, a strong partisan might really identify with Senator Elizabeth Warren as a political role model and fail to respond when I offer former secretary of state Hillary Clinton as a role model.[1] In either, very likely, scenario, my attempt to examine political role model effects would be at best dampened and at worst nonexistent—even though the person may, in fact, be impacted by a political role model, just not the one the study offers. Essentially, exposure to a political role model that has not been identified by the individual violates a primary tenant of ICT: role models must be personal.

Establishing causation also faces numerous other barriers. First, if the investigation is going to have external validity—the ability to generalize outside of the experimental condition—then there needs to be realism in the connection a study participant has with the role model figure in the study design. A meaningful encounter with a potential role model is challenging to contrive in a single experimental treatment, and natural experiments present challenges (and arguably ethical considerations) in capturing a meaningful control group that is not exposed to a role model or genuinely does not have a role model.

Second, role models, especially political role models, may have cumulative effects, an idea supported by the survey data in both Chapters 4 and 5. In Chapter 4, in the general population sample, fewer than one in six (15.9 percent) respondents indicated they had been connected to their self-identified political role model for less than a year, while more than 40 percent indicated the connection had been longer than five years. Among candidates for elective office (Chapter 5), even fewer reported more recent connections with their political role models; only 3.4 percent of role models reportedly were established in the previous year. If most people report prolonged attachments to their personally identified role models, a brief encounter is not likely to provoke the same magnitude of effect and perhaps would not inspire any role model effect whatsoever.

Additionally, the minimal effects from a brief, nonpersonal encounter may be limited by ceiling effects. For example, more than 80 percent of respondents in Chapter 4 said they voted in the 2020 election, and we know well the consequential impact of things like age, race, socioeconomic status, partisan attachment, and interest in politics (Verba, Schlozman, and Brady 1995) on voter turnout. These effects leave little room to detect what may be much smaller effects on voting—especially without large-N studies. The same is true for other forms of participation and political attitudes; role model effects may play a role, but that impact may be much less perceptible than factors that weigh heavy on people's political behavior and attitudes.

As such, I make numerous compromises in the two experiments I conduct in this chapter and in Chapter 7, and I expect that causation may still prove somewhat elusive because of the myriad challenges to experimental design. I also consider the moderating effects of the ICT relational factors discussed in previous chapters: the strength of the relationship with the role model (*known*), the duration of the relationship (*duration*), and the attainability of role model accomplishments (*attainability*). With the first experiment (Study 1) in this chapter, I seek to establish role model effects for a general population sample—as in Chapter 4, it also uses a Lucid Theorem sample. The second experiment (Study 2), which I discuss in Chapter 7, aligns with Chapter 5 and uses a sample of those considering running for political office (i.e., elite)—participants in a campaign training. This latter sample is composed of women, which allows for consideration of the inoculation effects theorized in ICT. I discuss Study 1 here before synthesizing the findings in the context of ICT and turning to Study 2 in Chapter 7.

General Population Role Model Effects

In this general population sample experiment, I give participants a choice of numerous high-profile political role models from those most frequently identified by the general population sample employed in Chapter 4. Respondents in that sample were apt to name a current or former U.S. president or some other high-profile national political figure. While it is quite likely that many participants in this experiment may identify with someone who does not appear in the list generated in Chapter 4, those results suggest that a majority will and that the remainder may be able to select someone they find sufficiently inspiring. This scenario, then, actually offers a more robust test of political role model effects. If the role models whom participants are exposed to are not necessarily the ones they would have chosen, finding role model effects from a merely sufficient figure is suggestive that the impact of role models may be even greater than these experimental results suggest.

I discuss this approach in more detail in the following, but it allows for me to test four primary hypotheses that serve to complement the findings in Chapter 4 about the impact of political role model effects in the general population. These hypotheses examine the two primary components of ICT. First, political role models have the potential to inspire political behavior and attitudes (motivational theory), and second, ingroup role models who share an individual's gender and/or race may pronounce this effect (inoculation theory). The first two hypotheses, then, examine motivation. The *Inspiration Hypothesis* asserts that people with political role models will be inspired to engage in politics by someone they identify as a role model. This hypothesis examines the normatively good aspects of political behavior and attitudes; it predicts that having a political role model will encourage voting and political participation, as well as political efficacy, trust, and perceptions of representation. As seen in Chapters 4 and 5, however, not all the attitudes associated with political role models are encouraging features of political citizenship. The *Inspiration Hypothesis* thus also predicts that the more negative attitudes that citizens may have (e.g., political aggression or support for political violence) will be lessened by positive role model effects. Specifically, it states the following:

> *Inspiration Hypothesis:* Americans will be *more likely* to report a willingness to participate in politics and express more positive political attitudes and *less likely* to express negative attitudes when exposed to an inspirational message from a political role model than

an inspirational message from a non–role model, an inciting message, or no message whatsoever (control). These differences will be moderated by contextual features of the role model relationship—attainability of the role model, how well known the role model is, and how long the aspirant has known the role model.

ICT also focuses on the role model orientation of the aspirant's relationship with the role model, so I also anticipate that the encouragement that an inspiring message from a role model offers will be impacted by how attainable that role model's status seems, how well known the role model is to the aspirant, and how long the aspirant has felt a connection to the role model. Generally, role model effects should be more apparent and more potent when the connection to the role model is stronger. In other words, positive role models—operationalized as "inspiring" in this chapter—are more likely to have a more pronounced impact if someone feels that they could achieve like the role model, they know the role model quite well, and this connection has persisted for some time.

The second hypothesis focuses more on the normatively negative aspects of potential political role model effects and how political role model effects may shape negative behaviors and attitudes. Despite a conflicted body of scholarship about whether negative campaign messages suppress voter turnout (see Ansolabehere and Iyengar 1995; Brooks 2006), Mann, Arceneaux, and Nickerson (2020) recently demonstrated that political participation (e.g., contacting an elected official) is not impacted by a negativity-tinged provocation. And, further, no research has examined the impact of how a role model message is framed—positive or negative. ICT suggests, however, that because role models have motivating power, they can provoke not just positive (inspired) behaviors and attitudes but also more negative ones. I test this more negative effect with a message that is inciting, thus operationalizing negative as "inciting." The idea here is not difficult to grasp; if someone you admire suggests you consider something in a more negative light, this is likely to cloud your view of that thing—especially if they are viewed as an authority in that area, as a political role model is likely to be in politics.

The *Incitement Hypothesis* tests the idea that people with political role models will be incited to political acrimony by someone they identify as a role model and that this negativity may serve to suppress the "good" aspects of citizenship that manifest as participation (e.g., voting or political participation) and positive attitudes (e.g., efficacy, trust, or positive perceptions of representation). It is as follows:

Incitement Hypothesis: Americans will be *more likely* to express negative attitudes and *less likely* to report a willingness to participate in politics or express positive political attitudes when exposed to an inciting message from a political role model than an inciting message from a non–role model, an inspirational message, or no message whatsoever (control). These differences will be moderated by contextual features of the role model relationship—attainability of the role model, how well known the role model is, and how long the aspirant has known the role model.

As the hypothesis outlines, and as with the expectation for positive role model effects, I anticipate these effects will be moderated by the three relational features of role models—attainability, known, and duration.

The subsequent two hypotheses test for the ingroup potency of these role model effects. As ICT predicts, because the connection with an ingroup role model may be especially relevant to the aspirant, we may see instances where individuals are more impacted by these relationships. These effects were difficult to examine in Chapters 4 and 5 because of small sample sizes, but the experimental design employed in this chapter has the potential to shed additional light on how marginalized citizens are inspired by their political role models. These hypotheses mirror those described prior; the Inspired Citizenship *Inspiration Inoculation Hypothesis* focuses, again, on the positive aspects of political engagement:

Inspiration Inoculation Hypothesis: People with ingroup political role models will be more inspired to engage in politics by someone they identify as a role model than someone inspired by an outgroup political role model or a person who is not a political role model.

On the more detrimental side of politics, the Inspired Citizenship *Incitement Inoculation Hypothesis* tests the idea that people with ingroup political role models will be more incited to political acrimony by someone they identify as a role model than someone incited by an outgroup political role model or a person who is not a political role model. This can be stated in these words:

Incitement Inoculation Hypothesis: Ingroup role models are more likely to encourage political aggression and support for political violence.

Data and Methods

I test these hypotheses by varying whether a participant receives an inspirational or inciting message from someone they chose to identify as a political role model or from an unidentified political leader, as well as a control condition where participants are not exposed to a message of any kind. Those who indicated they had no political role model and those who declined to select a role model from the available options were excluded from participation.[2] This allows me to isolate the impact of a political role model. The experimental conditions are seen in Table 6.1.

The experiment was conducted on the Lucid Theorem platform using Qualtrics software in October 2021. I removed 24 cases across all conditions of respondents who failed an attention check. This resulted in a total sample of 631 participants. The resultant sample was slightly more male (53.1 percent) and from the American South (39 percent), 29.2 percent BIPOC, and 51.3 percent Democrat versus 32.4 percent Republican (with 16 percent independent and leaning neither way).

Participants were first asked if they had someone they identified as a political role model, using the same question as in Chapters 4 and 5:

> Role models are people who, either by doing something or by being admirable to you in one or more ways, have had an impact on the political decisions you have made in your life. Role models may be people you know personally, or they may be people you simply know of. They may have had a positive influence on you, or they have had a negative influence. Is there anyone you would name as a political role model?

Those who indicated they had a political role model were sent to one of the conditions indicated in Table 6.1.

Conditions 1 and 2 prompted participants to select someone from a list of ten potential political role models. This list of political leaders was

TABLE 6.1 CONDITIONS FOR EXPERIMENTAL GENERAL POPULATION TESTING OF INSPIRED CITIZENSHIP THEORY			
	Political role model	Message	N
Condition 1	Participant selected	Inspiring	126
Condition 2	Participant selected	Inciting	115
Condition 3	n/a	Inspiring	134
Condition 4	n/a	Inciting	122
Condition 5	n/a	n/a	134

chosen because of the frequency with which the individuals were mentioned by the general population sample in Chapter 4. I also broadened the selection some to ensure racial, gender, and partisan diversity of role model options for the participants to select from. On one hand, this method does serve to perpetuate the practice in political science role models research of predetermining who the role models are or should be in our research, which I have thus far been critical of as a practice that facilitates the examination of role model effects rather than those stemming from descriptive representation. On the other hand, using the sample generated in Chapter 4 as a subject-driven way to determine likely role models offers a reasonable proximation of exposing participants to a person whom they themselves would identify. The ten role model options and the frequency of selection by participants are shown in Table 6.2.[3]

In Chapter 4, nine of these national political leaders were named as personal political role models, making up just over half of those named in the sample. The exception is Representative Cheney; she was not named by the Chapter 4 sample but was added to balance the gender diversity of the Republican options.[4] While which role model participants chose only mattered for whom they were told had delivered the subsequent speech, the selection frequencies mirrored those in Chapter 4. For example, two-thirds of the sample selected Presidents Trump, Obama, or Biden. The similarities in selection would seem to justify my approach in cultivating personally identified role models for the participants.

Once participants in these conditions selected their role model, they were directed to the experimental treatment. Participants read a brief speech, presumably recently delivered by their chosen role model but actually adapted from President Ronald Reagan's presidential farewell address in 1989 to bolster the external validity of the treatment. One version of

TABLE 6.2 STUDY 1 CHOICE OF POLITICAL ROLE MODEL OPTIONS	
Role model	N
President Donald Trump	65
U.S. Senator Tim Scott	4
U.S. Senator Bernie Sanders	25
Vice President Mike Pence	11
U.S. Representative Alexandria Ocasio-Cortez	19
President Barack Obama	54
Vice President Kamala Harris	16
United Nations Ambassador Nikki Haley	5
U.S. Representative Liz Cheney	5
President Joe Biden	52

the speech offered inspirational rhetoric, the other version inciting rhetoric. Those in conditions 3 or 4 read the same inspiring or inciting speeches, but unattributed. The excerpt from the speech read as follows:

> The lesson of the 2020 election was, of course, that because we're a great nation, our challenges seem complex. It will always be this way. But as long as we remember our first principles and believe in ourselves, the future will always be ours. Standing today in the shadow of the Washington Monument, I realize there is something else we have learned: Once you begin a great movement, there's no telling where it will end. If we believe that we can *come together to create/rise up to fight* for the government we want, if we are willing to *expend our time and energy as/willing to go up against fellow* Americans, we can change not just the nation, but the world. I want to encourage you to be willing.

After reading the speech, participants were asked, as in Chapter 4, about their political attitudes and political behavior. ICT would predict that there would be differences in how those exposed to encouraging messages from their personal role models compared to those who were exposed to those same messages without a role model connection and those in the control group who received no message.

Findings

Motivational Role Model Effects

These are not precisely the words Reagan delivered in his farewell address, but undoubtedly his speech was received differently by those who admired him as a political role model than by those who did not. Chapter 4 suggests that people with political role models tend to be more likely to vote (or at least report they do) and participate in politics. The survey data used in that chapter was able to identify that people with role models were more engaged but not necessarily that their role model played a role in encouraging that engagement, as I could not establish causation. It could be that those who are more engaged are just more likely to have role models, not that there are effects of having a role model. While that is a potentially interesting feature of political role modeling, it is not a role model effect per se. The experiments in this chapter allow me to test ICT's assertion that political role model effects include encouraging deeper political engagement.

In testing the first hypothesis, the *Inspiration Hypothesis*, I examine this causal relationship. I anticipated that those participants in the conditions where a selected role model offered inspiration would be more likely to vote and report more acts of political participation than those in the no-role-model and control conditions. There is very little variation in the sample with regards to their intent to vote in the next election. Almost the entirety (94.4 percent) of the sample said they were either somewhat or very likely to vote in the 2022 midterm elections. Since most people do say they intend to vote (whether they actually do or not), there is not much variation to examine in the voting measure. Differences between the conditions were thus exceptionally small and not statistically significant.

Main effects: Turning then to political participation, I look first at the main effect of a role model inspirational/inciting message. While voting does not wind up being a very amenable dependent variable, there is more variation to examine in the political participation index. This is the same index used in Chapter 4, and it was created by combining the four measures used in the American National Election Studies (ANES), only in this case, participants are asked to anticipate their participation in the next 12 months rather than retrospectively, as the questions are typically framed. Each activity is coded 0 for not anticipating they would participate in an activity in the upcoming 12 months and 1 if they anticipated they would participate, creating—when combined—a scale of 0 to 4. The participants, across conditions, reported prospective participation in an average of just over one activity ($\mu = 1.278$).

For political participation, however, I look at the individual acts of participation to better gauge where role model effects may exist and where they do not. Figure 6.1 shows the effect (Cohen's d) size between conditions (control, message only, and message from role model) for a respondent's anticipated participation in protesting, contacting an elected official, supporting a political candidate or cause, and donating to a political candidate or cause. As predicted, the effect sizes range from infinitesimally small ($d < .10$) to approaching medium ($d < .4$). These effect sizes (however small) are the role model effects.

I hypothesized that an inspirational message from a role model would encourage political participation as compared to an inspirational message with no role model association and a control with no message. More specifically, I anticipated that an inspirational message (no role model) would result in more anticipated participation than a control and that a role model delivery of that same message would increase anticipated participation even further. The results for inspiring messages (Figure 6.1, top) are mostly inconclusive. There are statistically significant differences between the

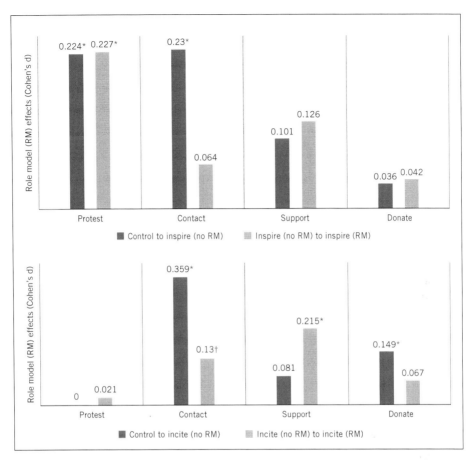

Figure 6.1 Role Model Effect Size on Anticipated Acts of Political Participation, Inspiring and Inciting Messages
(*Note:* *p < .005 significance determined by two-tailed t-tests.)

control condition and the messaging (no role model) condition for protest (p < .001) and contacting (p < .001), but both are in the opposite of the hypothesized direction—that is, the inspirational message is not inspiring political engagement. The same is true for supporting and donating to candidates, though neither of these reach statistical significance.

Intent to protest rebounds (though only back to levels identical to the control condition) with the addition of a role model delivering the inspirational message (p < .001); however, the other three forms of engagement are further depressed—though none of the three reaches statistical significance. The consistent suppression of anticipated participation across engagement types suggests the possibility that (1) participants did not find the delivered message inspiring, (2) respondents were discouraged by a message delivered by a political figure whether or not they identified the messenger as a role model, or (3) political participation is not susceptible to bolstering by role model effects, at least not by a brief exposure—or, of course, some combination of each of these three considerations.

The suppression of political participation hypothesized for the more negative inciting messages shows more evidence of a role model effect. Again, Figure 6.1 (bottom) shows the effect size among the control condition with no message, the inciting message (no role model), and the inciting message delivered by a role model. Here, also, effect sizes range from nonexistent ($d = 0$) to small ($d = .359$). Presenting an interesting contrast to the effects of an inspirational role model, where there is a statistically significant effect of the role model delivering the message, there is no effect of an inciting role model on protesting. The largest effect on political participation is the suppression of anticipated contacting from the inciting message, though this rebounds some—with marginal significance (though still not to the level of the control condition)—when a role model is delivering the message ($p < .066$).

The hypothesized pattern is most obvious for both supporting and donating to a candidate or cause. For both forms of engagement, respondents in the inciting-message (no role model) condition had lower anticipated engagement than in the control (though only donate was statistically significant, $p < .033$), and that engagement was further depressed by the addition of the role model, though here only support was statistically significant ($p < .001$).

The differences revealed between these conditions offer evidence for the existence of role model effects in support of the *Incitement Hypothesis*, which argues that role models have the potential to suppress political behavior when their messaging is negative. For contacting, supporting, and donating, the negative message appears to suppress anticipated participation—which is amplified by a role model effect when the negative (i.e., inciting) message is delivered by a role model.

Turning to political attitudes, I test the inspiring and inciting hypotheses for evidence of role model effects, as in Chapter 4, on efficacy, trust, and perceptions of representation. As with political participation, I test for a statistically significant difference between the aggregate mean of those in the control, message-delivery, and message-delivery-with-a-role-model conditions using two-tailed t-tests.[5] I then calculate Cohen's d effect sizes between conditions to isolate the role model effect. These effects sizes— the lighter bars again representing the isolation of the role model effect—

are illustrated in Figure 6.2 As with the analysis of role model effects on behavior, the Cohen's d values are, without exception, quite small.

Across the three attitudes I examined, there is some additional, tentative evidence in support of the *Inspiration Hypothesis.* The inspiring message appeared to make a bigger difference than the role model delivery of it, though many of the differences did not reach even marginal significance. With regards to efficacy, the inspiring message actually depressed participant political efficacy somewhat ($\mu = 2.46$ vs. $\mu = 2.29$), though this was not statistically significant. The addition of a role model delivering that same message, however, bolstered efficacy as compared to both the control and message-only conditions; this role model effect was marginally significant ($p < .10$).

Trust, on the other hand, was elevated by the message (also with marginal significance). While it was not further increased by the addition of role model delivery, the difference between the message-only and role-model-delivery conditions was very small and not significant ($\mu = .82$ vs. $\mu = .80$), suggesting that a role model could still be an effective way of boosting citizen political efficacy when delivering an inspiring message. A similar pattern existed for respondents' perception of representation, though these differences were not statistically significant.

As Figure 6.2 (bottom) reveals, the results for the role model effects on these same political attitudes have small differences between the control, message-only, and message-with-role-model-delivery conditions. The role model effects tend to be in the hypothesized direction (suppressed), but none reach statistical significance.

Note, however, that to this analysis I add an additional effect size to the examination of the reports of political aggression and support for political violence. Given the analysis in Chapter 4 that revealed the elevation on these measures among those who identified President Biden or President Trump as role models, I separate out those who selected either Biden or Trump as their role model and received an inciting message from them. These participants were much more likely to report having participated in acts of political aggression ($\mu = 2.05$ vs. $\mu = 2.54$, $p = .027$) in the condition where the inciting message was delivered by either Biden or Trump than if they just read the inciting message unattributed. While the role model effect size here is still small ($d = .336$), it is easily arguably large enough to be meaningful; it certainly strengthens the case that these political role models hold a distinct power to impact those who admire them.

Moderation: It should not be surprising that there is only limited evidence in support of the two hypotheses that guide this chapter, the *Inspi-*

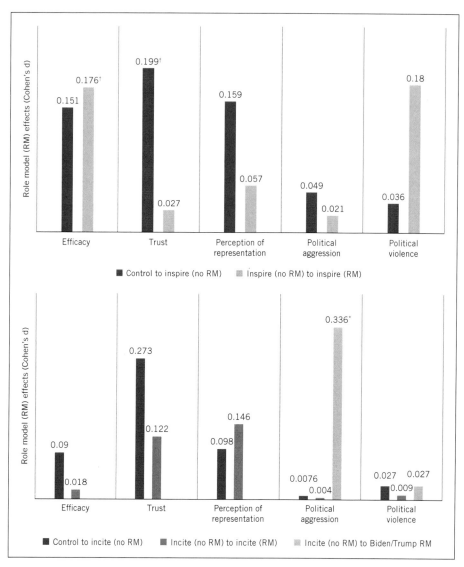

Figure 6.2 Role Model Effect Size on Political Attitudes, Inspiring and Inciting Message
(*Note:* Cohen's d; *$p < .005$; †$p < .010$ significance determined by two-tailed t-tests.)

ration Hypothesis and the *Incitement Hypothesis*. Both of these hypotheses, however, incorporate a consideration of ICT beyond that of the main effects discussed prior—that is, that the impact of political role models may be conditional upon features of the role model–aspirant relationship: how attainable the role model seems (*attainability*), how well known the role model is (*closeness*), and how long the relationship with the role model has existed (*duration*). In other words, a political role model whom someone feels a stronger connection with through these three features of the relationship is likely to have a stronger role model effect. I now turn to testing for how these three relational features moderate the impact of a political role model on political behavior and attitudes. For rigor (and simplicity), here I only report findings that meet conventional alpha levels ($p < .05$).

By virtue of the fact that only some subjects were randomly assigned to a condition with a role model, I can only examine how these factors moderate in two ways: (1) within subjects in that condition (for the strength of moderation) and (2) between the inspiring and inciting messaging conditions (for the difference in moderation). It should be noted that while these analyses add depth to my tests of role model effects, within-subject tests would point to correlational relationships, not causal ones like the between-subject tests have thus far. I continue to omit any analysis of voting due to the lack of variation in self-reported intent to vote.

I start by examining how these features of the role model relationship moderate the effect of an inspiring message delivered by a role model. Figure 6.3 reveals that how well known a role model is moderates ($p < .001$) an inspiring message's impact on projected political participation. The more known the role model is to the subject, the higher their anticipated level of political participation. In other words, when people are exposed to an inspiring message from a political role model of their choosing, their anticipated political participation is higher if that role model is better known to them than if the role model is less well known to them.

Turning to moderation analysis on political attitudes, I find evidence of moderation on four of the five attitudes I examine in this study. With regard to political efficacy, I find no evidence that the impact of an inspiring message delivered by a role model is moderated by the perceived attainability of the role model (*attainability*), how well known or close the role model is (*known*), or how long the participant has been connected to the role model (*duration*), as all three effects lie outside traditional levels of significance.

Known, however, moderates the relationship between the inspiring message and political trust, perceptions of representation, reports of political aggression, and support for political violence (Figure 6.4), though not entirely in support of the *Inspiration Hypothesis*. With political trust, *known* moderates ($p = .012$) in that the more known the role model is to the subject, the higher the subject's political trust (see top left of Figure 6.4). Additional support for the hypothesis is revealed by moderation analysis on the variable of perceptions of representation; *known* also moderates on this

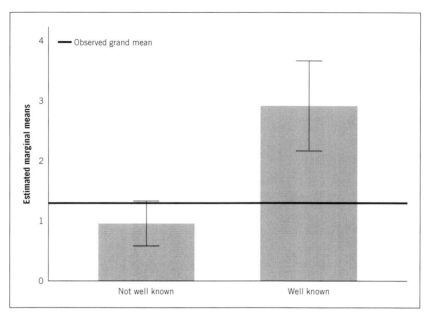

Figure 6.3 Estimated Mean of Political Participation with Inspiring Role Model Message Delivery, by Role Model Closeness
(*Note:* Interaction effects measured using a univariate general linear model; $p < .05$. Not well known $\mu = .977$, well known $\mu = 2.824$.)

variable, such that subjects who knew their role models more fully were more likely to think people like themselves are well represented across levels of government (see top right of Figure 6.4). *Known* also moderates the relationship between an inspiring role model message and a respondent's reports of political aggression ($p = .011$); however, this interaction actually increases reports of political aggression (see bottom left of Figure 6.4), contrary to the prediction of the *Inspiration Hypothesis*.

Unlike these other attitudes, when analyzing support for political violence, the interaction between an inspiring role model message and how well known that role model is falls just outside of statistical significance ($p = .054$); however, in this instance, the duration of the connection to the role model is statistically significant ($p = .050$) and moderates the relationship as the *Inspiration Hypothesis* predicts. The more enduring the aspirant's relationship with a role model, the less supportive of political violence the aspirant is (see bottom right of Figure 6.4).

In all, it appears that there is substantial support for the *Inspiration Hypothesis* seen through the lens of moderation analysis. Political participation and most of the political attitudes I examine are enhanced—

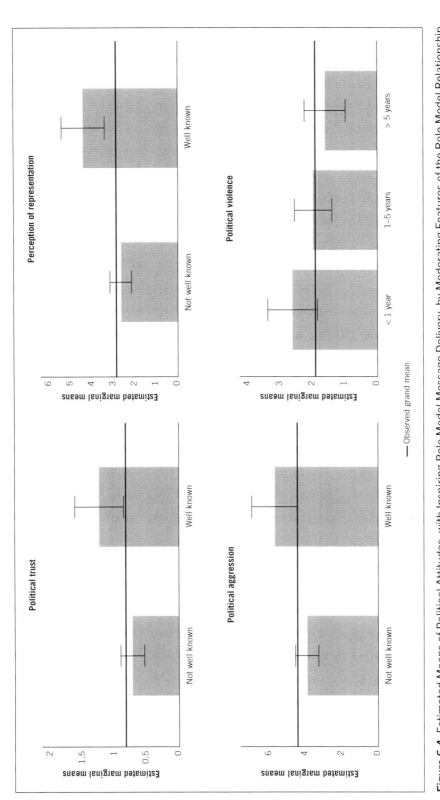

Figure 6.4 Estimated Means of Political Attitudes, with Inspiring Role Model Message Delivery, by Moderating Features of the Role Model Relationship

(*Note*: Interaction effects measured using a univariate general linear model; $p < .05$.)

more normatively positive—when individuals are exposed to an inspiring message from a role model they know relatively well.

Turning to examining how features of the role model relationship moderate the relationship between an inciting message delivered by a role model and political behavior and attitudes, I find a similarly important function served by *known* as a moderator, as well. As Figure 6.5 reveals, *known* again moderates the relationship between political participation and the inciting message. In this case, however, it contradicts the *Incitement Hypothesis*, and role models who are more well known increase participant claims of plans for future political participation.

Known again moderates in support of the *Incitement Hypothesis* ($p = .036$), which asserts that role model delivery of a negative (inciting) message will suppress feelings of efficacy. *Duration* fell just outside statistical significance ($p = .054$). Both *known* ($p = .020$) and *duration* ($p = .043$) moderate the relationship between an inciting message from a role model and political trust, though in opposite ways. *Known* increases trust as the role model is more well known, contrary to the hypothesized relationship. *Duration*, however, moderates as hypothesized, with those who have had a

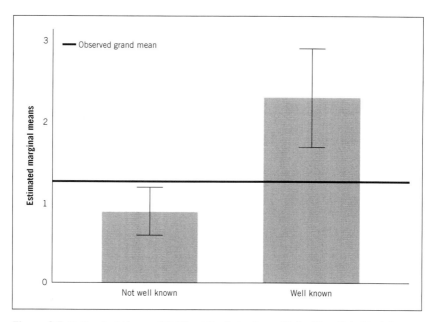

Figure 6.5 Estimated Mean of Political Participation with Inciting Role Model Message Delivery, by How Well Known the Role Model Is
(*Note:* Interaction effects measured using a univariate general linear model; $p < .05$. Not well known $\mu = .96$, well known $\mu = 2.421$.)

longer-standing relationship with the role model expressing lower levels of trust. The interaction between *known* and *duration* is also significant ($p = .008$), which is the relationship I show in Figure 6.6 (top right) to illustrate the nuance involved in this moderation. This reveals the pattern where, on average, those who have been connected to their chosen role model for longer periods do trust the government less, but knowing that role model better reduces that impact. *Known*, once again, moderates the relationship ($p < .001$) between an inciting message from a role model and perceptions of representation in the same positive way it did with an inspiring message, contradicting the relationship I hypothesized but suggesting that role models can have more normatively positive effects even when they may be delivering a somewhat negative message.

Turning to the more obvious tie between an inciting message and political attitudes, *known* moderates in support of the *Incitement Hypothesis* ($p = .003$) on reports of political aggression (see Figure 6.6, center right). A well-known role model delivering an inciting message (like an inspiring one unexpectedly did, as I discuss prior) provokes increased reports of political aggression than a not-well-known role model. Similarly, *known* moderates the relationship between the inciteful message and support for political violence ($p = .011$) such that when subjects read an inciteful message from a well-known role model, as opposed to one they do not know as well, they are more likely to support political violence (Figure 6.6, bottom)—as hypothesized.

Overall, this analysis reveals that how well someone knows[6] their role model is important, but the duration[7] of that relationship in some cases also moderates or—in one instance—creates a three-way interaction with how well known the role model is and role model delivery of the message. Notably, attainability appears to not have much of an impact as a moderator—despite having played a seemingly larger role in the survey data presented in Chapter 4. I suspect this is likely in part an artifact (or limitation) of the experimental design in this chapter that only presented participants with extremely high-level role model options, whereas there was more variation in the identified role models in Chapter 4. Furthermore, neither the inspiring nor inciting treatments on their face would provoke explicit attainability considerations. This experiment essentially does a better job of testing the closeness and duration features of role model orientation and less so the attainability considerations. This is obviously an area where further experimental investigation could help clarify the moderating effect of how attainable the role model's success may seem to the aspirant.

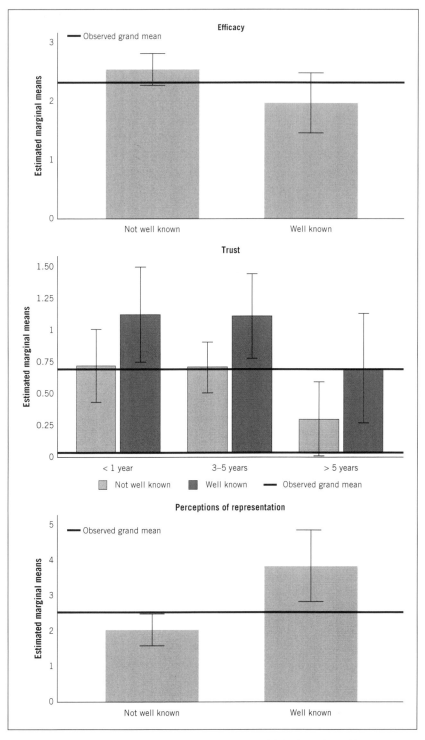

Figure 6.6 Estimated Means of Political Attitudes, with Inciting Role Model Message Delivery, by Moderating Features of the Role Model Relationship (*Note:* Interaction effects measured using a univariate general linear model; $p < .05$.)

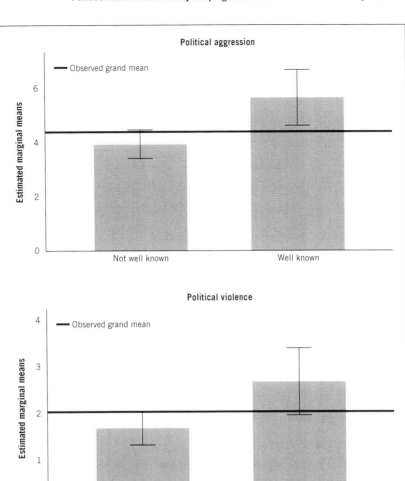

Figure 6.6 (*continued*)

It is not excessively important that the direction of the influence is consistent with the type of message being delivered since the goal of this work and ICT is not to test the impact of different types of messages, but rather the power of role models in delivering them. I am also in no way arguing that role model effects would be at all powerful in the context of the complex set of influences that impact political behavior and attitudes. I do, however, find small effects across virtually all of my outcome variables that suggest that role models do have the potential to influence citizens, especially in a more real-world environment where exposure to one's identified role model would likely be varied and sustained. There may be important unexplored ways messaging could control the positivity or negativity of those effects.

Inoculation Role Model Effects

I now turn to the inoculation effects that role models may have. These two hypotheses, the *Inspiration Inoculation Hypothesis* and the *Incitement Inoculation Hypothesis*, essentially predict that participants with ingroup role models will be more prone (than those with outgroup role models) to the effects of the inspiring/inciting messages delivered by their role models. Recall that participants chose from a list of both men and women who were white or BIPOC, primarily compiled from the individuals most frequently identified as political role models in Chapter 4 but with some augmentation to ensure a comprehensive set of high-profile women and men, Republicans and Democrats, and both white and BIPOC potential role models. Only participants who indicated they had a political role model were directed into treatment conditions.

From this list of potential role models (see Table 6.2, previous), 82.4 percent selected men and only 17.6 percent chose women, which is unsurprising given the apparent attraction of current and former presidents in the Chapter 4 data—all of whom are obviously men. Gender of participants was not necessarily predictive of the gender of their selected role model, especially for women, who only chose a female role model 21.7 percent of the time. Men chose male role models 82.4 percent of the time. The participants also predominantly chose white role models (61.6 percent) over BIPOC ones (38.4 percent). Race was predictive of a participant's choice of role model ($p < .05$),[8] though this was mostly driven by white participants' preference for white role models. White participants chose white role models 65.9 percent of the time, while 46.9 percent of BIPOC participants chose a BIPOC role model. Ultimately, a significant majority of participants shared at least one of their identities (race, gender) with their selected role model, with more than a third having a fully ingroup role model, sharing both race and gender with the individual they selected (see Figure 6.7).

Party affiliation is associated with whether a role model is likely to be an ingroup role model or outgroup role model ($p < .009$).[9] Republicans (46.4 percent) were much more likely than Democrats (28.8 percent) to share both their gender and racial identity with their role model, while Democrats were much more likely than Republicans to share neither identity (22.4 percent vs. 9.5 percent, respectively).

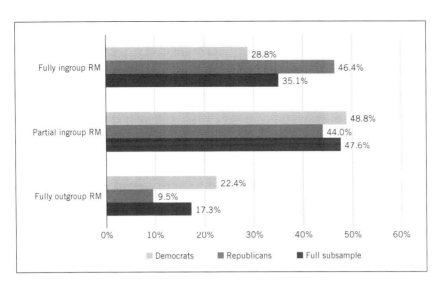

Figure 6.7 Percentage of Participants Choosing Ingroup, Partial Ingroup, or Outgroup Role Model

To determine whether messages from ingroup role models are more potent than outgroup ones, I conduct a series of OLS regression analyses on each of the six behavior and attitudinal dependent variables. I control for political party and type of message (inspire vs. incite), restricting the sample to only the conditions where participants heard a message from a selected role model ($n = 256$). ICT would suggest that the inoculation effects an ingroup role model can have would contribute to a stronger impact of the message being delivered.

First of all, the R-squared of these models are consistent with the impressions the effect sizes leave in the proceeding analyses: the impact of these considerations is modest at best. Furthermore, I do not find the type of message the participant received from the role model to be significant, so deciphering between the inoculation effects from the type of message—which is not really the intention of the analysis in this chapter anyway—is not really possible for any of the dependent variables.

However, the inoculation effect of ingroup role models does seem to be present for a majority of dependent variables. These are shaded in grey in Table 6.3. Having an ingroup role model encourages the aspirant to both report anticipating greater political participation ($p < .034$) and enhanced political trust ($p < .030$)—both of which are considered good for democracy. However, an ingroup role model also increases both reports of po-

TABLE 6.3 EFFECT OF INGROUP ROLE MODEL ON POLITICAL BEHAVIOR AND ATTITUDES

	Political participation	Political efficacy	Political trust	Perception of representation	Political aggression	Political violence
Inspire vs. incite	−.081 (.187)	−.081 (.147)	−.064 (.097)	−.109 (.271)	−.021 (.316)	.077 (.212)
Political party	−.154 (.194)	−.205 (154)	.288 (.101)***	.091 (.283)	.005 (.331)	−.067 (.220)
Ingroup role model	**.154 (.135)***	**−.065 (.107)**	**.149 (.070)***	**−.043 (.195)**	**.158 (.231)***	**.175 (.152)***
R^2	.030	.045	.095	.027	.024	.049

Note: Model run using OLS, ***$p < .001$, *$p < .005$. Ingroup role model coded as 0 = fully outgroup, 1 = partially ingroup, 2 = fully ingroup. Constant omitted in table for simplicity.

litical aggression ($p < .030$) and support for political violence ($p < .013$). For example, what this looks like in the bivariate relationships is that 4 percent more (11.1 percent vs. 7.1 percent) of those with fully ingroup role models report the highest levels of political participation, while 11.6 percent fewer of those with fully outgroup role models report the lowest levels of political participation (43.2 percent vs. 54.8 percent). That seems meaningful.

Similarly, in the bivariate relationships between in-/outgroup role models and support for political violence, there are 16.5 percent fewer participants with fully ingroup role models than fully outgroup role models who say they strongly disagree that political violence may be necessary (18.4 percent vs. 34.9 percent). The opposite is also true for those who strongly agree, with 10.2 percent more of those with fully ingroup role models stating they support violence this way (21.8 percent vs. 11.6 percent). In both cases, these findings point to the possible influence role models could have in turbulent political times—especially if high-profile role models chose to use that influence.

Conclusion

In this chapter, I addressed two primary considerations. First, I wanted to try to establish whether the associations between people with role models and certain patterns of political behavior and attitudes that I found in Chapter 4 were a result of people with role models having a quintessentially different orientation toward politics or if—as ICT would suggest—role models are capable of influencing political behavior and attitudes. The experimental evidence presented in this chapter probably does not violate the idea that people who identify with role models are different than those who do not, but it does point to role models having the capacity to influence their aspirants.

I consistently find evidence of role model effects, albeit frequently small ones, across most of the behaviors and attitudes I examine. An inciting (negative) message from a personal role model as opposed to the same message without a role model, for instance, mildly suppresses an individual's inclination to want to contact an elected official. Alternatively, an inspiring message from a role model—again compared to a message without a connection to a role model—increases feelings of political efficacy. This addresses the second primary consideration posed in this chapter: could role models be used in normatively positive ways to improve citizen orientations to American democracy?

The answer to this question appears to be yes, perhaps especially under two conditions well predicted by ICT: if the role model is well known and/or the role model shares the aspirant's identity. How well known the role model is to someone moderates the relationship between a message delivered by a role model delivered and most of the variables examined here, though not always in the hypothesized way.[10] For example, those who were exposed to their chosen role model articulating an inspiring message were more likely to report higher levels of political trust if they indicated they had a more deeply connected relationship with that role model. This is evidence that more well-known role models have the power to motivate their aspirants to have stronger political attitudes, as ICT would predict. It may point to why Presidents Trump and Biden had such potent effects in Chapter 4; it is not hard to have accumulated a lot of familiarity with individuals who have campaigned aggressively and been in the news as the leader of the country for years on end.

I also find evidence for the inoculation component of ICT that proved difficult to tease out in Chapters 4 and 5. In the experiment conducted here, when someone shared either a gender or racial identity, or especially both, with their role model, it worked to strengthen the effect of role model messages, though, again, not always having the positive effect I anticipated from inspirational messages or the suppressive effect I anticipated from inciting messages. Ingroup political role models, for example, seem to encourage people to think about being more politically active and more supportive of political violence. This makes intuitive sense, as partisanship has increasingly become a "super identity" (Mason 2018) that frequently divides along racial and, to a lesser extent, gender lines. When you are compelled to action by someone with whom you share many relevant identities, you are likely more likely to act—as ICT would also suggest.

In sum, role model effects are their own distinct phenomena in the consideration of political behavior and attitudes in the general population. Having established that there is likely some independent impact of political role models on the political behavior and attitudes of the general population, I now turn to examining the relevant components of ICT on political elites. Chapter 7 looks for experimental evidence that role model effects can impact the candidate emergence process as well.

7

See It? Be It?

Political Role Models Encouraging Political Candidacies

> I related to her path and what she did on that path; she speaks up and she speaks her mind; I don't always agree with what she says/does on city council but I respect how she presents herself, she does not come across angry or hateful.
>
> Demonstrated what tenacity can accomplish in achieving a political position, gave me confidence in myself to also attain a political job.
>
> —Campaign training participants, 2017

These comments were made about an elected official—a woman—who participated on a panel about navigating the state's political parties at a nonpartisan campaign training for women. When participants were asked to reflect on whom they had identified with as a role model during the training, many of them said similar things. They identified with someone during the training, admired the traits and skills their role model exhibited, and often mentioned after the training that they felt their role model's success seemed attainable.

For several years, I helped deliver a nonpartisan candidate training program for women in two major U.S. cities. The number who participated fluctuated from year to year, but typically 50–70 women would spend a very long Saturday learning about the nuts and bolts of running for office. I served as a logistical host or sometimes moderated a panel discussion, but for the most part, I was not the one who delivered the content to the program participants even though much of it would have been relevant for me to speak about. Role models did that work.

The idea was that others who had participated in the process and in most cases had run for office themselves would serve as more promising figures to inspire and educate the training participants. In many ways that seemed to be the case, as participants rated the program highly in their posttraining surveys, and many of them went on to run for political office. Many of them also won those races, with some coming back to participate in the program as panelists or speakers later.

My colleague Monica Schneider and I studied the effectiveness of these trainings and found that the trainings increased the confidence of the women who participated and made them think more positively toward a political career (Schneider and Sweet-Cushman 2020). While we cannot tie this impact directly to the use of role models, they are so ubiquitous in the training delivery that it is hard to imagine they are not part of the equation. At the very least, we know that in some cases, the role models used in campaign trainings could impact desired training outcomes (Sweet-Cushman 2018a).

These trainings, then, offer a natural experiment in which to further test ICT in an elite population. In Chapter 5, I surveyed individuals who ran for office in 2020 about their political role models and examined the associations between those role model relationships and their future intentions in electoral politics. This data revealed that former political candidates who professed to have political role models were different than those without role models. The former were more likely to feel a sense of belonging in politics, to win their races, and to be interested in running in the future. In this chapter, I offer an experimental field study on the impact of role models on a set of political elites who are not quite ready to be political candidates.

The use of role models in a campaign training helps illustrate how ICT may manifest in an applied environment in three ways. First, this training was designed for women considering a run for political office and primarily (though not exclusively) employed the use of potential role models who were also women. This means this use of role models is very directly applying the inoculation component of ICT. That the use of same-gender role models would be an effective means of bolstering women's interest in running for office makes infinitely intuitive sense. Research in social psychology suggests that role models, especially women, can be inspirational for women considering similar paths. However, there are considerations beyond just sharing a gender identity. In STEM, Fuesting and Diekman (2017) found that role model traits and orientation are crucial; in their words, "it is only when a female scientist is prototypic of her gender and the perceiver is highly communal-oriented that communal affordances are cued indirectly" (647). In politics, a communally framed scenario improved women's perception of a political career (Schneider et al. 2016), though the gender of the role model[1] did not seem to matter in the scenario (Schneider and Holman 2020).

Second, campaign trainings for women make gender salient. Evidence demonstrates that people are likely to find same-gender role models inspiring only when they are relevant (Lockwood and Kunda 1997). That these trainings use women who have explicitly followed the general path the aspirants are considering (as this chapter's epigraph illuminates) makes the role models and their gender relevant.

Finally, and most important to this chapter, ICT asserts that individuals need to be able to identify with a role model (Hoyt, Burnette, and Innella 2012) *and* believe the role model's success is attainable for their future self (Lockwood 2006). While those aspiring to political office may be starstruck and excited by exposure to a famous or high-achieving political role model, that success may feel out of reach and daunting (Hoyt and Simon 2011)—especially as they take the first big steps into a political career. I examine the attainability component of the role model context. This adds nicely to the experiments employed in Chapter 6, where we saw role model attainability had little importance in the general population. This is sound empirically given that most of those in the general population do not aspire directly to their role model's success, while nearly everyone in a sample of campaign training participants likely does to some degree.

I anticipate that even a brief exposure to a political role model will have the potential to impact the candidate emergence of someone considering running for political office, and in this context, making a political career seem attainable will be crucial. After all, attendees at a candidate training program have implied—by attending the program—that they have at least some interest in reaching the same exact type of success as the elected officials used as de facto role models in a training.

How Will Role Models Affect Women's Political Ambition?

It is important to note that traditional measures of women's political ambition (Lawless and Fox 2005, 2010) have proven notoriously difficult to enhance. We should especially expect women attending a training about how to run for office to already have substantially elevated levels of ambition. As such, ambition itself is subject to ceiling effects (Schneider and Sweet-Cushman 2020) in the context of a candidate training. Ambition may also provoke emergence in the short or long term or anywhere in between; there is no reason to treat each candidate's individual opportunity cost calculation as generalizable to any other candidates. Ambition, however, is also multifaceted, and candidate emergence almost certainly depends on factors above and beyond raw ambition. Some potential candidates might, in fact, feel less interested in a political career after learning more about what would be required through a campaign training program.

Nonetheless, I anticipate that a campaign training that relies heavily on the use of role models will elevate ambition and ambition-adjacent factors for women who identify with a role model in the training. ICT supports this expectation in two broad ways. The first is through the main effect of a role model as a motivator and inoculator, and the second is through the moderating effect of the nature of the role model relationship, such as the strength of identification and how attainable the role model's success appears. I test hypotheses for both these expectations.

For the main effect, ICT recognizes that role models can be motivating and that ingroup role models can be especially effective in inoculating against implicit and explicit expectations that the aspirant does not belong. In this case, women are chronically underrepresented in politics and may benefit from both the implicit message that women can have political careers and the explicit recognition of women who have found success in the profession. As such, the entire training constitutes a role model intervention:

> *Training Intervention Hypothesis:* Political candidate training for women that relies on the use of role models will elevate the ambition of those who identify with a role model during the training.

Arguably, however, role models are not the only aspect of a candidate training that might encourage women's interest in a political career. They are exposed to a greater understanding of what a political career looks like and substantial information about how to plan and execute a political campaign. Both these features (and countless others) might contribute partially or fully to changes noted in ambition and related factors. One way to get a sense for how much impact role models might be having in a training context is to examine the variation in how strongly the training participants identified with a role model. As mentioned prior, strength of identification with a role model is crucial to the impact of that role model (Hoyt, Burnette, and Innella 2012). Chapters 4, 5, and 6 all show—consistent with ICT— that people who identify with a political role model are different from those who do not. Here, I look within the strength of that identification for evidence that, as ICT would suggest, a stronger identification with a role model during a campaign training can amplify the effect of training:

> *Strength of Identification Hypothesis:* Participants in a political candidate training for women who identify more strongly with a role

model within the training curriculum will have more elevated ambition following the training than those with weaker identification.

And finally, participants in a campaign training may identify with a political role model whose success seems more distant and remote or with those whose success seems like something participants could more easily aspire to. According to ICT, this can impact aspirants' political behavior, especially their interest in running for political office, since in this case they are very directly attempting to emulate the behavior and accomplishments of the role model. This consideration of attainability is most important for political elites since the ability to emulate may be very clearly impacted by how attainable those goals are for the aspirant. I expect the perception of how attainable the role model's success is to matter:

> *Attainability of Success Hypothesis:* Campaign training participants who identify with role models whose success seems more attainable will report greater increases in ambition following the training, as compared to before.

Campaign Training Field Experiment

I use a field experiment to test these hypotheses.[2] As part of the team that delivered the Ready to Run nonpartisan campaign training for many years in two locations in Pennsylvania, I was able to survey women attending the training in 2017 before and after their exposure to potential political role models. The use of role models is a purposeful, though not explicit, component of these trainings. Successful women—mostly current or former elected officials themselves—serve as speakers and contributors throughout the daylong training.

The conditions were not conducive to a true experiment, as participants could not be assigned, randomly or otherwise, to a control condition that did not employ any potential role models to deliver the content. Because the training constitutes a treatment and features one crucial element of experimental design—pre-post testing—the research design is aptly quasi-experimental. This should inspire some skepticism about the absolute causation embedded in the findings, but this is likely as close to a true experiment as is possible in the context of campaign trainings given ethical considerations about making sure all participants are exposed to the content that would promote cultivating candidate emergence.

Prior to the training, and then again following, participants were asked to complete a paper questionnaire. The pretest established participant baselines on eight ambition and ambition-adjacent measures. The posttest asked participants whether or not they felt any of the speakers throughout the training constituted someone they would consider a political role model, utilizing the same language used to prompt role model identification throughout the rest of this book. Again, note that while participants were limited to select a role model from those who had participated in the training, the selection was participant selected rather than researcher driven. This is critical to the application of ICT, which emphasizes the importance of individually identified role models.

Of the participants in the two cities, 198 completed either a pretest or a posttest; 75 (37.8 percent) completed both,[3] a good response rate given the difficulties similar studies report collecting elite samples (see Bernhard et al. 2019). Of these, 88 percent ($n = 66$) indicated they identified with someone from the training as a role model, almost identical to the percentage of candidates in Chapter 5 who reported having a role model. I use only these participants to conduct the forthcoming analyses. The sample skewed Democratic and as mostly strong partisans, as might be expected for those who are considering running for office in a state with a strong party system like Pennsylvania but also likely elsewhere, too, given the state of partisanship in the United States. None of the respondents had ever held elective office in the past. Race was the only statistically significant demographic variation between the two training sites; one training site included a statistically higher percentage of women of color ($p <$ .001),[4] though the overall small sample size does not allow for any analyses by participant characteristics.

Training Outcome Variables

Practitioners who organize and deliver campaign trainings usually tend to do a satisfaction-type survey following the training, but program evaluation or outcome measurement are rare. It is also difficult to track participants' political careers and even more difficult to attribute any success that might be had to a training experience, especially a one-day training like the one examined here. Critics and supporters of various campaign trainings are also unlikely to agree what constitutes a "successful" program.

Political scientists, however, have been attempting to measure political ambition and studying candidate emergence intently, especially among women, for approaching two decades. I draw on these measures, extensions of these measures along a future continuum, and a handful of other measures that are frequently associated with candidate emergence. In all, I examine eight outcome variables that range from whether participants have ever thought about running for office (*ambition [thought]*) to whether they see themselves imminently running for office (*ambition [next year]*) to how likely they are to run at some point in their lives (*ambition [lifetime]*). Each of these was measured both before and after the training.

Two features of the political role model relationship are relevant to this analysis: identification and attainability. The other two role model relationship variables considered in applying ICT up until this point, how well known the role model is and the duration of the role model relationship, are arguably not relevant in the context of this experiment. Since all the participants in the training had the same exposure for the same amount of time to everyone they could identify with as a role model, there is theoretically no variation in these attributes of the role model relationships.

Role Model Identification

After being asked to reflect on and name a role model from the day's training, respondents were asked about the strength of identification with their role model (see Lockwood 2006)—this becomes the variable *identify*.[5] I have previously published work (Sweet-Cushman 2018a) that combined this variable with two others that in this context are more accurately analyzed as measures of attainability. I combine these two additional variables, (1) how likely they are to obtain similar success and (2) generally how obtainable the role model's achievements are, both of which are on 7-point scales,[6] to form the variable *attainability*. The means on both these success measures were relatively high, which is unsurprising given that 70 percent of those who identified a role model listed someone who was not a high-level role model (i.e., a congresswoman who gave the keynote address). I split this attainability variable into high and low categories at the mean to create a binary variable that provides easier interpretation; lower levels of attainability equal 0, and higher levels of attainability equal 1.

Findings

I treat the full campaign training as a role model treatment. While it may vary some in other trainings, Ready to Run (all of them, to my knowledge) uses people well positioned to be considered role models in the political realm. Role models may not be the most potent force in a campaign training experience, but there is no empirical evidence that the content matters more than who delivers it. Regardless, these trainings are a sustained exposure to role models—an incredibly difficult thing to otherwise manipulate.

To test the *Training Intervention Hypothesis*, I use paired-samples t-tests to determine if the mean values of the training outcome variables are significantly different posttraining than they are pretraining. The pre- and posttraining means of each of the eight training outcome variables are shown in Table 7.1.

Five of the eight ambition variables see no meaningful change from before the training to after the training, again acknowledging the ceiling effects that come from an already motivated sample, but three other outcome variables do. These are shaded in grey in Table 7.1. One of the ambition and the two ambition-adjacent variables do increase posttraining ($p < .05$). *Ambition (future)*, which asks participants to categorize the likelihood of them ever running for office in the future, is arguably the most open-ended of the ambition measures and thus perhaps the most realistic measure of potential for candidate emergence. The increase seen here pre- to posttraining ($\mu = 1.16$ vs. $\mu = 1.31$) pushes the participants overall closer to running for office being "something I might do in the future." There are also positive improvements pre- to posttraining on what I have so far called the ambition-adjacent measures—that is, the two training outcome variables that are not specifically asking about running for office but rather about thoughts anticipating a political career. Participants' views of a political career are more positive posttraining ($\mu = 5.24$ vs. $\mu = 5.71$), and they are more confident that they would be successful in politics ($\mu = 5.49$ vs. $\mu = 5.75$). To the extent that the mechanism at play here is the impact of the use of role models during the training, there is some evidence of positive impact on women's potential candidate emergence when role models are employed. I now turn to providing more evidence for role model effects in this context by more directly investigating the impact of individually identified role models.

TABLE 7.1 CANDIDATE TRAINING OUTCOME VARIABLES MEASURED PRE- AND POSTTRAINING

Measure	N	Pretraining mean	Posttraining mean
Ambition (future)	51	1.16	1.31*
Ambition (thought)	56	2.39	2.43
Ambition (next year)	53	2.74	2.74
Ambition (five years)	51	4.76	4.76
Ambition (ten years)	50	5.80	5.72
Ambition (lifetime)	50	6.06	6.04
Perception of political career	55	5.24	5.71*
Likelihood of successful political career	55	5.49	5.75*
Note: Paired-samples t-tests with Bonferroni correction for multiple tests, *$p < .05$.			

Strength of identification with the participant's professed training role model was quite strong, with a mean of 5.41 on a 7-point scale. The *Strength of Identification Hypothesis* suggests that the stronger the identification, the more positive impact the training will have. There is already evidence that this is true. In preliminary analyses I published several years ago (Sweet-Cushman 2018a), I looked at only the *ambition (future)* and *ambition (thought)* variables and found a positive correlation between strength of identification and these measures, though only *ambition (thought)* was statistically significant. Here, though I am limited by sample size, I add substantial complexity to the analysis to look at the function of role model identification more closely.

In comparing the means of the net change in each variable from pre- to posttraining (see Figure 7.1), there are two things that stand out. First, for those with both higher and lower strength of identification with their

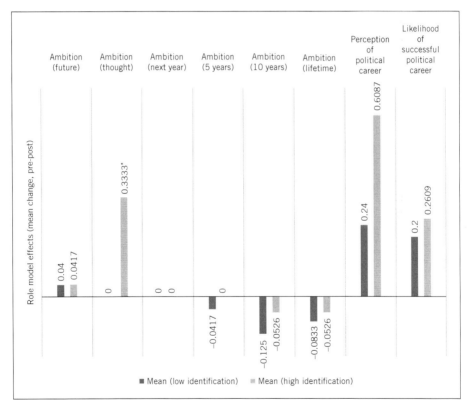

Figure 7.1 Mean of Net Change (Pre-Post Training) of Training Outcome Variables, by Strength of Role Model Identification
(*Note:* Independent samples t-test with Bonferroni correction for multiple tests, *$p < .05$; variables are on a 3-point scale. *Ambition [future]* is on a 4-point scale.)

training role model, the mean change is zero in many cases, suggesting that these were not variables impacted by the training regardless of role models or identification with them.

The second thing to note in Figure 7.1 is that every single variable is in the hypothesized direction. Those with stronger identification (high identification in Figure 7.1) experienced either more positive change in their training outcomes or less negative change where the participant mean was overall negative. The exception is, understandably, *ambition (next year)*, which asked participants if they anticipated running for office in the upcoming year, which, it should be noted, was incredibly unlikely to be changed by the training, which was held only about four months before the state's primary election. While these findings are suggestive of a broader impact of role model identification, only *ambition (thought)* (the "softer" of the general ambition measures) reaches statistical significance ($p = .021$), with those with stronger role model identification, on average, moving closer to having "seriously considered" a run for office while those with lower (weaker) identification, on average, had no change in their consideration. A practitioner who organizes campaign trainings, I dare say, would be thrilled to see that much movement in a measure of nascent ambition!

Finally, I examine the difference in the mean changes pre- and post-training on a number of the training outcome variables by higher and lower levels of *attainability* to test the final hypothesis. The *Attainability of Success Hypothesis* predicts that when training participants feel that the accomplishments of their role model are accessible to themselves and others, they are more likely to have been more encouraged to consider running for political office by their experience at the training. Again, I use independent-samples t-tests to determine if the mean change between pre- and posttraining differs for participants who perceived the attainability of their role model differently (low vs. high attainability); these results are shown in Figure 7.2.[7]

A similar pattern emerges in testing this attainability hypothesis as did for the identification hypothesis. There are, again, not surprisingly some instances of zero mean change between the pre- and posttest values. However, with the exception of *ambition (ten years)*—how likely participants felt that they would run for office in the next ten years—all the values were in the hypothesized direction. In other words, those who reported sensing their training role model's success was seemingly attainable had more positive changes or, alternatively, less negative ones in the case of *ambition (lifetime)*. At the same time, those who saw the role model's accomplishments as less accessible had more negative or less positive changes as a result of the training.

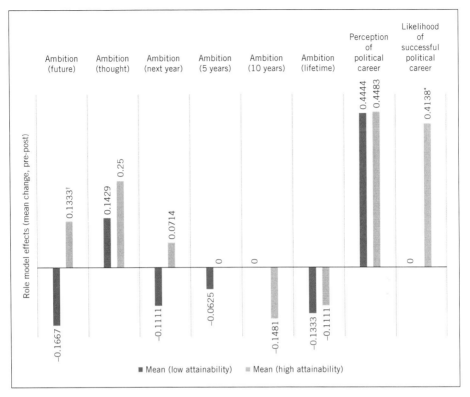

Figure 7.2 Mean of Net Change (Pre-Post Training) of Training Outcome Variables, by Perception of Attainability of Role Model Success
(*Note:* Independent samples t-test with Bonferroni correction for multiple tests, *$p < .05$, †$p < .10$; variables are on a 3-point scale. *Ambition [future]* is on a 4-point scale.)

Of course, while the pattern displayed here looks holistically support-ive of the *Attainability of Success Hypothesis*, only *likelihood of a successful political career* ($p = .046$) is statistically significant, though *ambition (fu-ture)*, which leaves a timeline completely open-ended for running for office, is close ($p = .094$). Again, this still offers excellent insight to practitioners, who seemingly would be wise to consider how overwhelming the accom-plishments of their speakers might be to newcomers to electoral politics.

Conclusion

Some of the hundreds of women who have come in and out of the cam-paign trainings I have helped organized show up for their training expe-rience absolutely set on running for office. They know what race they are running in and have already started to put together a campaign plan and structure. They are the exception. The vast majority come in looking pretty hesitant and feeling uncertain. Some, though definitely not all, of those women end the day with a much more confident sense of their political futures. Anecdotally, participants frequently say that they felt a connection to a training presenter and that the presenter made the possibility of running for office seem real to them. The training information and materials may prepare them, but the mechanism for further encouraging them to run? That sure seems to be the role model they identified with. Role model effects matter.

Empirically, there is evidence that campaign trainings bolster women's intent to run for office. Sanbonmatsu and Dittmar (2020) found that while many women come to a campaign training already posed to run for office, the training improves other participants' interest in running for elective office or seeking appointive office. Schneider and Sweet-Cushman (2020) similarly found that campaign trainings for women improve feelings toward a political career, especially in that they see politics as more congruous with their goals than they did before the training. Both these studies examined Ready to Run, which employs a role model structure for content delivery.

In this chapter, I used the same campaign training environment as a role model intervention in order to test the assumptions of ICT in the context of both political elites and those who are historically marginalized in the context of political representation: women attending a campaign training. ICT here would predict that women in this environment would likely identify with a political role model and that the strength of that identification, as well as how attainable the role model's success felt to the aspirant, would impact interest in running for office.

Indeed, training outcome goals include considering the impact of training on various measures of political ambition at different intervals of future time. The training also enhanced factors that could impact interest in running for office, like a positive perception of a political career. Given the emphasis on using role models to deliver training content in the campaign training I study, I use the training as proxy for a role model treatment. To the extent this is a reasonable understanding of the mechanism of pre-post change on training goals, I find ambition (at some undetermined point in the future) to be elevated, perceptions of a political career to be more positive, and an increased sense of the likelihood of success in a political career. And, importantly and consistently with the elites in Chapter 5, most participants reported that they identified with someone during the course of the training who embodied a personal role model.

When I examine the variation in how strong those identifications are, I find that most identified quite strongly with the role model. And, as ICT would predict, those stronger identifications are linked with more positive change in training outcomes. Specifically, participants with stronger identification were more likely to think about running for office than those with weaker identification.

Similarly, ICT predicts that role model effectiveness—especially for potential candidates—also hinges on how attainable the aspirant views the role model's success to be. Too high achieving and similar success might feel out of reach (Lockwood 2006), and, of course, too low and the person would not really be considered aspirational enough to even be a role model. Aspirants are Goldilocks-esque this way; they like their political role model's success to be *just right*. This is exactly what I find in the context of this training. Interestingly, both those who felt their role model's success was more attainable and those who thought the success was less attainable seemed to have the same increase in a positive view of a political career, but those identifying with a role model with more attainable success were more likely to believe they would be successful. They were also more likely to feel more inclined to run for office at some point in the future. According to ICT, this is precisely how political role models should work.

Overall, what testing role model effects in this context tell us is that for someone underrepresented in American politics[8]—in this case women, including women of color—who may be considering a political candidacy, a sustained exposure to a political role model can make a difference in how they feel about running for office. Inspiration to run or more seriously consider running is enhanced by features of this role model relationship, how strong the identification with the political role model is, and how attainable their success appears. As one participant wrote about the role model she identified with during the training: "(She) overcame adversity in male-ruled political world and achieved success at many levels. It made me feel like I could, too." That is ICT in a nutshell.

8

Political Role Models Good, Politicians Bad?

You can't have a better role model, a better mentor in this business than a Gwen Moore.

—State Assemblyman Supreme Moore-Omokunde

In 2004, U.S. Representative Gwen Moore became the second woman to represent Wisconsin in Congress and the state's first African American member of Congress—a path for which she credits her mother. Moore is also mom and political role model to her son Supreme, who in 2020 ran for and won a seat in Wisconsin's state assembly. He credits his mom (Dabruzzi and Small 2022). Having politically active parents, as I discussed in Chapter 3, is associated with higher levels of engagement for the child (Cicognani et al. 2012, Andolina, Jenkins et al. 2003). Assemblyman Moore-Omokunde was fortunate to have such a political role model for his entire life (*duration*), who was so close to him (*known*), whose accomplishments were so ubiquitous that he knew he could tackle that path too (*attainable*), and who defied the odds as a person of color (*racial ingroup*). Assembly Moore-Omokunde is quite the "inspired citizen."

Most of us, however, do not have Representative Moore as a mom. And, unfortunately, most of us are not gal pals with our city councilmember, though I highly recommend it. And almost no one is going to spend a very long Saturday learning more about how to run for office. In fact, much of America does not seem to have much use for the "politicians" who would fill these role model roles.

In 2017, *U.S. News & World Report* published a piece by Kenneth T. Walsh in which he lamented, in light of the Trump presidency, "how few public figures seem worthy of admiration by young people or anyone else."

Walsh (2017) pointed out how many people greatly esteemed Franklin Roosevelt or Ronald Reagan while it seems unfathomable that many would admire contemporary political figures with such fervor. Indeed, they do not. Toward the end of 2021, YouGov collected data on the most well-known politicians alive today. Former presidents Barack Obama (D) and George W. Bush (R) topped the list, followed by Bill Clinton (D), with 98, 97, and 97 percent "fame," respectively. Despite being known by virtually all Americans, they are not particularly popular. Obama is the most popular politician in America . . . at 57 percent; Bush and Clinton are much farther behind at 39 and 40 percent (YouGov, n.d.). Not exactly resounding endorsements for those positioned to be our most obvious political role models.

And it is not even just that individual politicians are failing to inspire Americans. Likely in response to the increased negativity in politics, the ANES started asking a question in 2016 that prompted respondents to indicate whether they agreed or disagreed that "politicians are the main problem in the United States" (see Figure 8.1). It seems profound that at that point almost 44 percent of respondents agreed. It seems even more profound that only four years later, this percentage had increased still (American National Election Studies, University of Michigan, and Stanford University 2017, 2021).

This all paints an ominous picture for our ability as Americans to admire individual politicians enough to see them as role models or even look to them for inspiration. It also suggests that the mere existence of in-

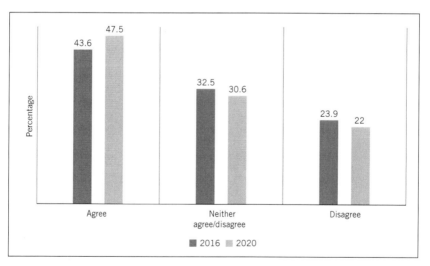

Figure 8.1 Percent Who View Politicians as the "Main Problem" in the United States, 2016 and 2020
(*Note:* Data from the ANES in 2016 and 2020.)

dividuals who are positioned to be political role models may never be sufficient to inspire aspirational political behavior like voting and acts of political participation or to impact political attitudes like efficacy and trust.

ICT nonetheless recognizes the power of role models to impact citizens, given the right circumstances. The mere presence of a potential role model in politics may be sufficient for some; after all, even former U.S. representative Tom Delay (R-TX) (who was indicted and convicted, though that conviction was later overturned, of criminal money laundering) has 14 percent favorability (YouGov, n.d.). However, this approval may have— or very much may not have—remained buoyed by his performance on the television show *Dancing with the Stars* in 2009.[1] But as ICT argues, the potential to inspire is magnified by how well known the role model is to the aspirant, and for how long, and how attainable their accomplishments seem to the aspirant. Seemingly, if Americans are willing and have the opportunity to connect more deeply with role models they identify with, those role models still hold the potential to inspire even in times when no one likes politicians.

Summary of Findings: People with Political Role Models Are Different, and Role Model Effects Are Real

ICT is both an extension and an integration of what is known about role models in social psychology. The two main streams of theory, MTRM (Morgenroth, Ryan, and Peters 2015) and SIM (Dasgupta 2011), lay a solid foundation for political behavior and attitude emulation and perhaps change based on a role model connection. ICT anticipates, based on MTRM, that Americans who identify with political role models will be politically different than those who do not. It also anticipates, based on application of MTRM in an abundance of nonpolitical contexts, that there are features of the role model relationship that are essential to the cultivation of role model effects. These include the strength of identification, how well known the role model is, how long the relationship has existed, and whether the role model's behavior/success seems like it could be successfully emulated.

The first question this book addresses with this framework is *who are our political role models?* We see ICT apply in Chapter 4 when a little more than half (52.1 percent) of the sample of everyday Americans reported that they had someone they recognized as their political role model, though some groups—notably white Republican women—are less likely than other groups to identify with a role model. Most of those with role models said they looked to a national political figure for inspiration, with U.S. presidents dominating the list; nearly one-third of those with role models named one of the last three presidents as their role model (presidents Biden, Trump, and Obama).

What is most obvious in examining the political behavior and attitudes of those in the general population who have political role models and those who do not is that those with political role models are very different types of citizens. This gives us insight into the second question I have been exploring in this book: *how do role models impact who participates in politics in America and how they do it?* Even controlling for obvious factors such as political interest, those who identify with a political role model are more likely to be politically active. They are, for instance, more likely to contact their elected officials or participate in a political protest. They are also more likely to have normatively positive political attitudes. Someone who identifies with former president Barack Obama, for example, likely has more trust in government. In fact, those with political role models had twice as much trust in government than those who did not. However, it should be noted that even the inflated trust of those with political role models was still objectively low.

These differences also carry over into more negative political attitudes as well. Both reports of political aggression and support for political violence are associated with having a political role model. This phenomenon is most notable among those who identified with the most recent party standard-bearers, Presidents Joe Biden and Donald Trump, who seem to be associated with support for political violence at disturbingly high levels. Anecdotally, it would seem that the January 6, 2021, Capitol insurrection was in a large way influenced by those who deeply admired former president Donald Trump. This real-life scenario can thus be at least partially understood with ICT.

A major contribution of ICT is that it prompts us to think not just about whether role models are important and who they are, but also about the context of relationships with role models by recognizing that the strength of identification is crucial to role mode effects. In this general population sample in Chapter 4, we see the importance of two of these features of role model relationships: role model familiarity and attainability. In both instances, the stronger the connection, the more citizens with role models stand out from those without.

ICT also points to the importance of ingroup role models as having the potential to "inoculate" citizens against forces of marginalization that might otherwise suppress their participation and/or attitudes about government. While I was somewhat limited by a small sample of BIPOC participants, I did find that having a political role model who is a member of the same gender and racial ingroup is associated with a greater likelihood of voting, more political participation, and more positive perceptions of representation. Ingroup political role models were also more likely to be associated with political aggression and political violence. I am not, however, able to separate out ingroup identification among those with marginalized identities. Nonetheless, most people were more inclined to identify with someone with whom they shared at least one identity, and this points to the possibility that there at least could be an inoculation effect—especially compared to those who do not have political role models at all.

Chapter 5 extends the application of ICT to political elites by addressing the third primary question of this book, *how do role models impact who runs for political office and why?* I examine how candidates for political office relate to role models and, again, how those who report having a political role model differ from those who do not. By centering the importance of role models to civic life, the theory would predict that more elites would identify (and more strongly, for longer, etc.) with political role models and that those relationships would be associated with more positive outcomes for the candidates. Indeed, Chapter 5 reveals that people who are willing to run for elective office are in many predictable ways different than those in the general population. Elites exhibit a much greater tendency to identify with role models. These individuals have high levels of connection with role models both using an adapted role models assessment scale and in their identification of their role models. Interestingly, here—as opposed to Chapter 4—Republican women candidates are among the most likely to have strong connections to political role models. In fact, it seems the groups in the general population most likely to identify with role models are the political candidates least likely to identify with them and vice versa.

However, despite some identity-based variation, a vast majority of political candidates identify with a political role model. Almost 82 percent named someone who was a political role model, but—again unlike the general population sample—they named a more diverse set of role models whom they tended to be closer to. At the same time, these candidates felt the accomplishments of their identified role models were harder to emulate. It appeared that—on the whole—attainable success of role models was actually associated with lesser likelihood of winning, but I would not be the first to point out that plenty of political candidates are not exactly realistic about their chances of winning, and plenty of candidates run knowing they will not.

What was most interesting, I think, was that perception of attainability of the role model's success did predict whether candidates thought they would run again. Those with role models, and especially those with role

126 / Chapter 8

models whose success seemed attainable, were more likely to say they would run for office again. Of course, ICT would suggest both this difference between those with and without role models and the differences—based on role model success attainability—within those with role models.

Inoculation effects were more difficult to discern among political candidates. One antithetical finding was that BIPOC male candidates with outgroup role models felt a greater sense of belonging in politics than those with ingroup role models. The lack of high-profile potential ingroup role models no doubt complicates this, but this warrants further investigation.

Both Chapters 4 and 5 reveal powerful associations between having a political role model, especially one with whom the connection is strong in some way, and political behavior and attitudes. Observational data, however, leaves us without a sense for whether role models have the capacity to change behavior and attitudes or if people with political role models are just quintessentially different than those without. The latter is, itself, an important contribution to political psychology and our understanding of civic life, but it does not add to the ongoing conversation in political science about role model *effects*. Exploring role model effects in political science is also of significant interest. Chapters 6 and 7 tend to these questions of causality in role model effects.

In Chapter 6, I draw on an original experiment to evaluate whether role model effects exist. In the experiment I designed, subjects were exposed to either a normatively positive (inspiring) or normatively negative (inciting) message from their chosen political role model or without any attribution. The space between the effect of the message and the effect of the message when delivered by a political role model is a precisely measured form of role model effect. Nowhere else in political science has such precision been applied to the measurement of role model effects. This role model effect was often nonexistent in both the positive and negative conditions, though not universally so. Where it existed (and was statistically significant), it was modest. However, it was—in fact—the first evidence I am aware of indicating of a true role model effect, although arguably in a very small intervention.

These effects became more prominent when I considered the moderating effects of the duration and the closeness of the role model relationship. How well known the selected role model was to the subject seemed to especially have an impact on political behavior and political attitudes. Having an ingroup role model also independently bolsters many measures, including political participation and trust in government, as well as reports of political aggression and support for political violence.

Finally, Chapter 7 offers the most promising evidence of the inoculation component of ICT. Because I look only at women—many of whom were women of color—in this chapter, I find evidence of how overtly ingroup role models can illicit role model effects on the potential for women to pursue a political career—noting, of course, that political ambition is hard to cultivate in anyone and even harder to elevate as it edges dangerously closer to actually running. Nonetheless, the purposeful use of female role models in a campaign training showed some evidence of role model effects, especially on feelings toward a political career (if not actually immediately pursuing one).

Candidate training outcomes traditionally examine movement on measures of prospective ambition at several future intervals and concepts related to a political career that are precursors to ambition. As I reveal here, and my colleague Monica Schneider and I have published elsewhere (2020), the training as a whole impacts participants' future ambition, perceptions of a political career, and evaluations about whether they would be successful in a political career. Participants in the training who identified a role model from within the training tended to identify quite strongly with their chosen role model—which itself, ICT would tell us, is setting the stage for role model effects.

Indeed, stronger role model identification was associated with more positive outcomes in every instance that there were changes from pretraining to posttraining. The largest gains as a result of the training were in the more ambition-adjacent measures—positivity toward a political career and belief of success in a political career—which is not unexpected given the ceiling effects inherent to ambition in those with already elevated interest in running. Attainability of the role model's success also had an impact on outcomes. Those who saw their role model's success as more feasible felt encouraged about their own potential success and did have more of a shift toward more concrete consideration of running for office in the future. These are, in most cases, small differences, but because I am looking at differences within those who have role models, they rightly should be. This field experiment is valuable beyond just the causal evidence of role model effects that it provides, as it also offers an applied use of role model effects that may have tangible effects for a population that has been historically marginalized in electoral politics.

Future Research

Of course, my work here has numerous limitations that should and could be refined and expanded by future research. First, in retrospect, a larger sample size of people who are not white could have been insightful for a number of analyses I would like to have done, especially in examining inoculation effects. Future research should consider how ingroup role models may be important across and within various identities. It is very probable that ingroup effects are different for politically dominant white men than for others who are politically marginalized. It is also infinitely likely that there are variations within those who identify as BIPOC. It is unfortunate that resource limitations so often, as they did in this project, limit the ability to parse these various differences.

Relatedly, one of the more interesting findings throughout the empirical chapters of this book is the lack of political role models among general population white Republican women and the relative abundance of role model identification within this same group for political elites. There is an obvious opportunity to refine ICT to consider the availability of potential role models in the consciousness of the average citizen as a factor that leads to lesser or greater role model identification and thus susceptibility to role model effects. The contrast between white Republican women in the general public and among candidates for office hints at an interesting potential refinement that I must leave to future investigations. In this same vein, I obviously focus only on adults in both general population and elite samples, but the power of socialization is so rich in one's younger years that broadening what little we know about political role models among young adults, adolescents, and children could be both insightful and valuable to the development of citizenship.

Research could also continue to examine different dependent variables that may be susceptible to role model effects or exhibit major variation between those who have role models and those who do not. The dependent variables I examine in this book offer insight into a sample of important political behaviors, and arguably are the more often studied, but certainly others have the potential to be relevant in understanding the breadth of impact role models might have on political behavior. Future work on voter turnout could incorporate work on role model effects. Campaigns seem to think high-profile surrogates can inspire people to turn out to vote, which is essentially a role model effect *if voters identify with them as such*. Different measures that gauge the connection between role model exposure and voter turnout may capture whether this strategy is effective.

Similarly, there is a universe of political attitudes that are important to civic engagement and identity in the United States. If these can be improved upon, or if we could understand how role models might be suppressing civic potential, we should investigate it. For example, in the contentious political times we live in, examining the impact role models can have on out-partisan affect has the potential to be more than just intellectually interesting.

I would greatly like to see research delve more deeply into particular political role models. The brief analysis I offer in Chapter 4 of support for political violence among those who identify President Biden and former President Trump as role models only vaguely breaks the surface of the potential that exists here. Is there specific rhetoric that cultivates positive and negative role model effects, for example? Would recognition of one's position as a political role model change the behavior of the role model? Again, expanding our understanding of how and when certain political figures connect with citizens—and candidates, among other potential groups— has value for cultivating healthier democratic norms associated with role models. ICT is more focused on the impact on aspirants, but we should endeavor to more fully understand the role models in the equation as well.

There are also unlimited considerations for how we might otherwise consider the application of ICT in everyday politics. How could we cultivate closer connections with positive political role models in children? Could elected officials cultivate stronger role model attributes by—for example—considering the way they communicate their success to seem more attainable? Could campaign professionals or political parties glean nuggets of valuable information that might aid in generating campaign ads or rhetoric that better position their candidate as a potential role model? Could those who conduct campaign trainings more purposefully choose role models with attainable success or more familiarity to participants? Could they change their curriculum to feature role models more overtly? I hope I have scratched the surface with the theoretical and empirical foundations I have laid in this book, but I recognize that I actually have more questions now than when I began this delve into better understanding the psychology of personal political role models.

Finally, this study does not speak to the potential persistence of role model effects, and I acknowledge this is a major limitation. While it appears that those with role models are different than their role model–free counterparts both in society and as candidates/potential candidates, there are questions about how temporary these results from exposure to a political role model might be. Are the subjects from Chapter 6 already less receptive to political violence than they were after they were exposed to a role model who was using inciting language, and if so, how long did that elevated support last? Did any of the women included in the study in Chapter 7 go on to run for office, or are they less uncertain about their political futures than they were after their training experience? We should get a better sense for the longevity of role model effects.

Implications of Findings

While there are a host of ways that the findings about political role models in this book are both theoretically and practically important, here I try to classify them into five broad categories that represent an important way of understanding how political role models function in American society.

First of all, people with political role models are different in some pretty notable ways. Before we even get to the point where role models might impact citizen behavior or attitudes, we can recognize that certain Americans are more likely than others to have role models. Those who identify with a role model are much more engaged and have more positive attitudes about government. For example, my data reveals that—in a general population sample—those who said they identify with a political role model also trust the government almost half the time. Of these respondents to my survey, 49 percent felt they could trust the federal government to do what was right always or most of the time. In the 2020 ANES (American National Election Studies, University of Michigan, and Stanford University 2021), that same percentage was not even 15 percent. Similarly, ANES reports that 8.4 percent of the general population participated in a protest in the previous 12 months. For those with role models in my sample, that number was nearly three times higher.

Ultimately, there is likely a feedback loop at play here. The more engaged you are in politics, the more likely you are to be exposed to individuals you may connect with as role models. Our interest might more appropriately be in those who do not have role models. Is it possible that—as a society—we could be more purposeful about providing opportunities for people to connect with political role models? Should we, for instance, make a more concerted effort to expose young people to individuals in the political sphere whom they could aspire to emulate? Whether it be teachers or parents or places of worship determining how political role models might be more deeply used in their environments, consideration should be given to the moderating factors described in this book. How can those of us concerned about the health of American democracy help others form new connections with political role models that persist, show evidence of attainable success, and encourage role models to become well known to citizens who would benefit from it?

Second, ICT promotes the idea of cultivating a more diverse set of potential role models. The data I have shared demonstrates we need to especially emphasize diverse role models, which would allow kids and adults to connect in a meaningful way to someone who looks like them, thus serving to inoculate them against the effects of marginalization. The demographics of those who do not identify with a role model in my sample connect so very clearly to the demographics of those who are generally underrepresented in politics. If you cannot see it, you cannot aspire to it. We need more diversity in high-profile political positions so that potential role models are more plentiful and visible. This means we need to continue to beat the drum, as I always do, about supporting candidates who represent underrepresented populations.

For example, given the tendency for people to connect with recent U.S. presidents in my sample, a female president of either party could perhaps serve as a role model to those who do not view themselves as identifying with one. The same could be true for other intersectional identities that I do not examine in this book, such as disabled or transgender Americans.

What I am calling for would foster a larger pool of potential political role models, but ultimately this pool would also provide descriptive representation. Recall that descriptive representation is not a sufficient condition for role model effects to occur. This book has demonstrated that political role model effects are real, distinct from descriptive representation, and at play in both positive and negative ways in the American electorate for both the general population and political elites. We should be careful how we attribute role model effects and make sure we are using that terminology properly.

In considering true role model effects, we should evaluate whom we elect as potential role models, and those who are elected should consider their potential to influence people more critically. To this point, I am reminded of an ad the Hillary Clinton campaign aired during the 2016 campaign that featured her opponent, Donald Trump, making violent references and saying unconscionable things about immigrants, women, and differently abled people, among others. Throughout the ad, young children were shown watching Trump deliver these now infamous lines. At the end of the ad, Clinton tells viewers that the country's children and grandchildren are watching. She asks, "What example are we setting for them?" The ad is titled "Role Models."

You should not have to agree with Clinton's politics to agree that we should be electing people who set a good example for our children and for the country as a whole. The effect of a role model could be to make someone feel more efficacious as a citizen, or it could be to aid an individual's acceptance of violence. Candidates and elected officials should be cultivating the former while rejecting the latter. Voters should reject candidates who do not.

Relatedly, finally, and most hopefully, there is the potential to use role model effects in normatively positive ways to improve democratic ideals.

Given that a large swath of the population connects with a president as a role model, presidential campaigns and administrations, as well as others positioned in political role modeling positions, should take note. The words these individuals use and the way they behave can influence millions of Americans. With democracy in a fragile place in the contemporary United States, its people must be handled with care. Political leaders should be attempting to inspire, not incite.

Conclusion

A discussion in my undergraduate political psychology class recently left me thinking about political role models. The students were expressing frustration with political activism and rhetoric from celebrities. While there were some dissenters, the students mostly wanted pop culture icons and political figures to remain two distinctly separate groups. They seemingly had little interest in emulating the political behavior or attitudes of their favorite actors, musicians, or sports stars. I would have been more surprised by this before writing this book. Virtually no one in my data collection listed someone from outside politics as a political role model. Our political role models come from inside politics.

ICT, then, does not pertain to our relationships with Taylor Swift or Simone Biles, regardless of how political they may choose to be. It applies to the mostly high-profile political figures we, as Americans, personally feel connected with. ICT also, as I have demonstrated, acknowledges how, in order to have potent effects (either positive or negative) on the general public and political elites, these role models need to be well known to their aspirants, have sustained connections, and—especially for political elites— have accessible components of their success.

As I have attempted to cultivate this theory, I have learned that we do not all have political role models, but those who do are more engaged—in positive and negative ways. I have learned that the impact of role models is more than just that those who have them tend to be different kinds of citizens. There is also the possibility of role model effects, too, and I have offered evidence of them impacting both political behavior and political attitudes in incremental ways with everyday citizens and those most engaged in electoral politics. There is a lot we do not know about what political role models can and cannot affect, but hopefully ICT offers a new way of leaning into those questions in the future.

In the meantime, I will continue to invite my friend and political role model, Councilperson Strassburger, to talk to my classes from time to time to inspire my students.

Appendix

TABLE A.1 IMPACT OF POLITICAL ROLE MODEL AND ROLE MODEL RELATIONSHIP ON PERCEPTION OF REPRESENTATION

	Model 1 (full sample)	Model 2 (role model only)	Model 3 (role model only)
Role model (Y/N)	.107*** (.099)	–	–
Role model attainability	–	.283*** (.020)	.267*** (.022)
Role model closeness	–	–	.071† (.042)
Role model duration	–	−.027 (.093)	−.045 (.097)
Observations	1418	772	726
R^2	.107	.171	.194

Note: The outcome variable is the number of political activities reported in the last 12 months. The variable ranges from 0 to 4, and I estimated each model using OLS models. Standard errors in parentheses. †$p < .10$, *$p < .05$, **$p < .01$, ***$p < .001$. Only variables of interest shown; remainder of model includes political interest, political participation, age, education, gender, race, and political party.

TABLE A.2 IMPACT OF POLITICAL ROLE MODEL AND ROLE MODEL RELATIONSHIP ON POLITICAL TRUST

	Model 1 (full sample)	Model 2 (role model only)	Model 3 (role model only)
Role model (Y/N)	−.046† (.022)	−	−
Role model attainability	−	−.260*** (.022)	−.234*** (.023)
Role model closeness	−	−	−.096** (.063)
Role model duration	−	.083* (.098)	.096** (.102)
Observations	1418	772	726
R^2	.243	.187	.268

Note: The outcome variable is the number of political activities reported in the last 12 months. The variable ranges from 0 to 4, and I estimated each model using OLS models. Standard errors in parentheses. †$p < .010$, *$p < .05$, **$p < .01$, ***$p < .001$. Only variables of interest shown; remainder of model includes political interest, political participation, age, education, gender, race, and political party.

TABLE A.3 IMPACT OF POLITICAL ROLE MODEL AND ROLE MODEL RELATIONSHIP ON POLITICAL EFFICACY

	Model 1 (full sample)	Model 2 (role model only)	Model 3 (role model only)
Role model (Y/N)	.104*** (.066)	−	−
Role model attainability	−	.296*** (.013)	.260*** (.013)
Role model closeness	−	−	.122*** (.037)
Role model duration	−	−.083* (.058)	−.094 (.060)
Observations	1418	772	726
R^2	.213	.301	.310

Note: The outcome variable is the number of political activities reported in the last 12 months. The variable ranges from 0 to 4, and I estimated each model using OLS models. Standard errors in parentheses. *$p < .05$, **$p < .01$, ***$p < .001$. Only variables of interest shown; remainder of model includes political interest, political participation, age, education, gender, race, and political party.

TABLE A.4 IMPACT OF POLITICAL ROLE MODEL AND ROLE MODEL RELATIONSHIP ON POLITICAL AGGRESSION

	Model 1 (full sample)	Model 2 (role model only)	Model 3 (role model only)
Role model (Y/N)	.049† (.097)	−	−
Role model attainability	−	.119*** (.023)	.083* (.024)
Role model closeness	−	−	.108** (.067)
Role model duration	−	−.081* (.104)	−.086* (.108)
Observations	1418	772	726
R^2	.206	.208	.212

Note: The outcome variable is the number of political activities reported in the last 12 months. The variable ranges from 0 to 4, and I estimated each model using OLS models. Standard errors in parentheses. †$p < .010$, *$p < .05$, **$p < .01$, ***$p < .001$. Only variables of interest shown; remainder of model includes political interest, political participation, age, education, gender, race, and political party.

TABLE A.5 IMPACT OF POLITICAL ROLE MODEL AND ROLE MODEL RELATIONSHIP ON POLITICAL VIOLENCE

	Model 1 (full sample)	Model 2 (role model only)	Model 3 (role model only)
Role model (Y/N)	.056* (.077)	–	–
Role model attainability	–	.156*** (.016)	.124*** (.017)
Role model closeness	–	–	.139*** (.046)
Role model duration	–	−.249*** (.073)	−.153*** (.075)
Observations	1418	772	726
R^2	.163	.243	.259

Note: The outcome variable is the number of political activities reported in the last 12 months. The variable ranges from 0 to 4, and I estimated each model using OLS models. Standard errors in parentheses. *$p < .05$, **$p < .01$, ***$p < .001$. Only variables of interest shown; remainder of model includes political interest, political participation, age, education, gender, race, and political party.

TABLE A.6 IMPACT OF ROLE MODEL ORIENTATION ON LIKELIHOOD OF WINNING 2020 CAMPAIGN

Role model attainability	.868† (.086)
Role model closeness	.879 (.203)
Role model duration	.8232 (.233)
Incumbency	.008*** (.544)
Major party	.770 (.708)
Gender	2.007† (.481)
Race	.902 (.557)
Observations	1031
Pseudo-R^2	.743

Note: The outcome variable is whether the candidate won his or her 2020 race. The variable is coded 0 = lost and 1 = won, and I estimated each model using binary logistic regression models. Odds ratio reported; standard errors in parentheses. †$p < .10$, *$p < .05$, **$p < .01$, ***$p < .001$.

TABLE A.7 FACTORS ASSOCIATED WITH A GREATER LIKELIHOOD OF HAVING AN INGROUP ROLE MODEL

Perception of representation	−.023 (.040)
Win	.039 (.211)
Party	.142 (.129)
Incumbency	.090 (.201)
Belonging	.010 (.017)
Gender	.278* (.118)
Race	−.209* (.124)
Observations	726
R^2	.113

Note: The outcome variable is how many identities are shared between the role model and the candidate, with higher values denoting more ingroup traits. I estimated the model using a linear regression model. Coefficients reported; standard errors in parentheses. *$p < .05$.

TABLE A.8 IMPACT OF INGROUP ROLE MODEL ON LIKELIHOOD OF WINNING 2020 CAMPAIGN

Ingroup role model	1.309 (.255)
Role model attainability	1.120** (.04)
Role model known	1.180† (.091)
Role model duration	1.205 (.120)
Incumbency	59.6934*** (.469)
Major party	4.195** (.498)
Gender	.804 (.249)
Race	1.533 (.336)
Observations	1031
Pseudo-R^2	.458

Note: The outcome variable is whether the candidate won his or her 2020 race. The variable is coded 0 = lost and 1 = won, and I estimated each model using binary logistic regression models. Odds ratio reported; standard errors in parentheses. †$p < .10$, *$p < .05$, **$p < .01$, ***$p < .001$.

TABLE A.9 IMPACT OF INGROUP ROLE MODELS ON BELONGINGNESS

	Model 1	Model 2
Ingroup gender role model	.015 (.496)	.015 (.540)
Ingroup race role model	−.131* (.499)	−.145* (.551)
Role model attainability	–	.130* (.074)
Role model known	–	.159* (.192)
Role model duration	–	.077 (.222)
Win 2020	.156* (.637)	.103 (.669)
Incumbency	.130 (.859)	.097 (.938)
Major party	.072 (.575)	.601 (.611)
Gender	−.068 (.429)	−.060 (.462)
Race	.013 (.501)	.014 (.546)
Observations	559	559
R^2	.103	.148

Note: The outcome variable is an index variable of four measures of belongingness that creates a 0–16 scale. Larger numbers on the scale imply a greater sense of belonging, and I estimated each model using OLS regression. Coefficient; standard errors in parentheses. *$p < .05$, **$p < .01$, ***$p < .001$.

Notes

CHAPTER 3

1. This is, objectively, a more significant political commitment than in the United States, where we do not really join political parties as much as identify with them.

2. Despite scientific evidence casting doubt upon the effectiveness of humanitarian measures employed by celebrities to aid those struggling in developing nations.

CHAPTER 4

1. After collecting participant responses, I removed from the data those who did not seriously respond to the open-ended questions about their role models, which served as a form of attention check. I removed those who indicated they had a political role model but whose responses did not specifically list a recognizable name of a person or left this blank. I also removed participants who had, in some cases, listed no role model despite claiming to identify with a role model or used traits to describe the role model that were not recognizable as potential role model traits. Those who indicated they had no political role model were removed from the data if they then used a specific person's name to describe their role model—indicating that they had failed to properly read the question asking about whether they had a role model. Whether they claimed to have a political role model or not, anyone who entered nonsensical information into an open-ended question had their full set of responses removed from the dataset.

2. Respondents were asked the following question adapted from social psychology by Sweet-Cushman (2018a): *Role models are people who, either by doing something or by being admirable to you in one or more ways, have had an impact on the political decisions you have made in your life. Role models may be people you know personally, or they may be people you simply know of. They may have had a positive influence on you,*

or they have had a negative influence. Is there anyone you would identify as a political role model?

3. A 14-point scale, μ = 8.3; Cronbach's alpha .747.

4. This variable combined responses to separate questions that asked respondents if they have a relationship with the role model, have met the role model, or have seen them speak in person. A 3-point scale, μ = .971, Cronbach's alpha .765.

5. Unfortunately, income data was not available for participants.

6. μ = .88; Cronbach's alpha .704.

7. Cronbach's alpha .799.

8. Respondents were asked, *How much of the time do you think you can trust the federal government in Washington, D.C., to do what is right?*

9. Respondents were asked, *How much can people like you affect what the government does?*

10. A scale variable that combines respondent reports of insulting, threatening, or inflicting physical violence on others because of their politics. The scale is 0–9, with larger values representing more incidents of aggression.

11. Respondents were asked how much they agree with the following statement: *Because things have gotten so far off track, true American patriots may have to resort to violence in order to save our country.* The scale is 0–4, with larger values representing greater agreement.

12. There was not enough variation outside the gender binary to conduct analyses beyond "women" and "men," which is a limitation of this research.

CHAPTER 5

1. Adapted from Nauta and Kokaly 2001; (R) indicates reverse coded items.

2. Cronbach's alpha .902.

3. Question text reads as follows: *Role models are people who, either by doing something or by being admirable to you in one or more ways, have had an impact on the political decisions you have made in your life. Role models may be people you know personally, or they may be people you simply know of. They may have had a positive influence on you, or they have had a negative influence. Is there anyone you would identify as a political role model?*

4. Motivation battery from Deckman 2007. All items had a response scale of not at all important (0) to very important (2).

5. Chi-square test of association with Bonferroni correction.

6. Interest in running for higher office is measured from 0 (it is something I would absolutely never do) to 4 (I definitely would like to do it in the future).

7. Since white men had no fully outgroup role models, and for ease of explanation, here I combine partial ingroup and fully outgroup role models into a single category.

CHAPTER 6

1. Indeed, despite the abundance of research that emerged following the 2008 and 2016 presidential election cycles that examined candidate Hillary Clinton positioned as a role model, she was barely mentioned by respondents in responses from either dataset utilized in Chapters 4 and 5.

2. There is no reason to expect role model effects among those who reject a role model; rather, my comparison group is those who did not reject a role model but were not exposed to one.

3. This table is included primarily for context. Recall that in each condition, participants received the same message, just ostensibly delivered by their chosen role model.

4. It seems reasonable to note that Cheney had, at this point, not emerged quite so significantly as a polarizing political figure within the Republican Party.

5. I corrected for multiple tests throughout this chapter with the Bonferroni test.

6. *Known* is not to imply a necessarily personal relationship but rather how familiar the aspirant is with the role model. This measure is generated from four separate questions—*Do you know this role model?*, *Have you met this role model?*, *Have you heard this role model speak in person?*, and *Do you regularly read or watch footage of this role model?*—each of which is a yes (1) or no (0) question. The sample mean was 1.5302. I recoded these so that 0–2 was considered not well known and 3–4 was considered well known.

7. *Duration* is measured on a 4-point scale: 0 = I do not have a connection to this role model, 1 = less than one year, 2 = three to five years, and 3 = greater than five years. For analyzing *duration* as a moderator, I exclude 0 from the analysis.

8. Pearson's chi-square test of association.

9. Pearson's chi-square test of association.

10. It should be noted that the distinction between positive (inspiring) messages and negative (inciting) ones is merely a tool to test for role model effects and not at all the focus of this chapter or this book. Meaning, then, that findings that run contrary to the hypothesized direction but are nonetheless significant are nonetheless role model effects.

CHAPTER 7

1. Again, I argue throughout this book that role models are not role models unless an aspirant has identified them as such. This study, like many others, more aptly presents *potential* role models.

2. I would be remiss to not acknowledge my friend, colleague, and frequent collaborator Monica Schneider here. She was instrumental in the design of this experiment for use in other contexts.

3. After a long day of training, it was difficult to get training participants—many of whom had completed the pretest—to complete both the training program evaluation and the posttest.

4. Chi-square.

5. These measures ask (each on a scale of 1 to 7, with 7 being most strongly) how strongly the respondent identifies with the role model.

6. Cronbach's alpha .799.

7. Note that this figure and Figure 7.1 show mean pre-post training *changes*, which means that the lower identification group may have started the training with higher levels of ambition, etc., or vice versa, and same for the divisions by attainability. I do not show those values because they are not relevant to examining the role model effects encapsulated in the training, as *the change is the role model effect.*

8. It goes, perhaps, without saying that Pennsylvania women are decidedly under-represented.

CHAPTER 8

1. Worth the watch: "Tom DeLay Storms Dancing with the Stars!," TPM TV, video, September 21, 2009, https://www.youtube.com/watch?v=epZlsCTNegwz.

References

Abbasianchavari, Arezou, and Alexandra Moritz. 2021. "The Impact of Role Models on Entrepreneurial Intentions and Behavior: A Review of the Literature." *Management Review Quarterly* 71 (1): 1–40.

Addis, Adeno. 1996. "Role Models and the Politics of Recognition." *University of Pennsylvania Law Review* 144 (4): 1377–1468.

Ahn, Janet N., Danfei Hu, and Melissa Vega. 2020. 'Do As I Do, Not As I Say': Using Social Learning Theory to Unpack the Impact Oof Role Models on Students' Outcomes in Education." *Social and Personality Psychology Compass* 14 (1).

American National Election Studies, University of Michigan, and Stanford University. 2017. *ANES 2016 Time Series Study* (ICPSR36824.v2, data file and codebook). Available at https://doi.org/10.3886/ICPSR36824.v2.

———. 2021. *ANES 2020 Time Series Study* (ICPSR36824.v2, data file and codebook). Available at https://doi.org/10.3886/ICPSR38176.v1.

Andolina, Molly W., Krista Jenkins, Cliff Zukin, and Scott Keeter. 2003. "Habits from Home, Lessons from School: Influences on Youth Civic Engagement." *PS: Political Science and Politics* 36 (2): 275–280.

Andolina, Molly, Scott Keeter, Cliff Zukin, and Krista Jenkins. 2003. *A Guide to the Index of Civic and Political Engagement.* College Park, MD: Center for Information and Research on Civic Learning and Engagement.

Ansolabehere, Stephen, and Shanto Iyengar. 1995. *Going Negative.* New York: Free Press.

Ashe, Jeanette, and Kennedy Stewart. 2012. "Legislative Recruitment: Using Diagnostic Testing to Explain Underrepresentation." *Party Politics* 18(5): 687–707.

Axon, Rachel, and Josh Salman. 2021. "They Rioted at the Capitol for Trump. Now, Many of Those Arrested Say It's His Fault." *USA Today*, February 10, 2021. Available at https://www.usatoday.com/in-depth/news/2021/02/10/trump-blamed-capitol-riot-some-who-were-arrested/4361411001/.

Bandura, Albert. 1969. "Social-learning Theory of Identificatory Processes." In *Handbook of Socialization Theory and Research*, edited by David Goslin. New York: Rand McNally and Company.

———. 1986. *Social Foundations of Thought and Action: A Social Cognitive Theory*. Englewood Cliffs, NJ: Prentice-Hall.

———. 1997. "Editorial." *American Journal of Health Promotion* 12 (1): 8–10. Available at https://doi.org/10.4278/0890-1171-12.1.8.

———. 2001. "Social Cognitive Theory: An Agentic Perspective" *Annual Review of Psychology* 52 (1): 1–26.

———. 2021. "Analysis of Modeling Processes." In *Psychological Modeling, Conflicting Theories*, edited by Albert Bandura, 1–62. New York: Routledge.

Barnes, Kristen. 2016. "Breaking the Cycle: Countering Voter Initiatives and the Underrepresentation of Racial Minorities in the Political Process." *Duke Journal of Constitutional Law and Public Policy* 12 (2): 123–178.

Basow, Susan, and Karen Glasser Howe. 1980. "Role-Model Influence: Effects of Sex and Sex-Role Attitude in College Students" *Psychology of Women Quarterly* 4 (4). https://doi.org/10.1111/j.1471-6402.1980.tb00726.x.

Bauer, Nichole M. 2020. *The Qualifications Gap: Why Women Must Be Better than Men to Win Political Office*. Cambridge: Cambridge University Press.

Beaman, Lori, Raghabendra Chattopadhyay, Esther Duflo, Rohini Pande, and Petia Topalova. 2009. "Powerful Women: Does Exposure Reduce Bias?" *The Quarterly Journal of Economics* 124 (4): 1497–1540.

Beaman, Lori, Esther Duflo, Rohini Pande, and Petia Topalova. 2012. "Female Leadership Raises Aspirations and Educational Attainment for Girls: A Policy Experiment in India." *Science* 335 (6068): 582–586.

Beck, Paul Allen. 1977. "The Role of Agents in Political Socialization." In *Handbook of Political Socialization Theory and Research*, edited by Stanley Allen Renshon, 115–142. New York: Free Press.

Beck, Paul Allen, and M. Kent Jennings. 1982. "Pathways to Participation." *American Political Science Review* 76 (1): 94–108.

Becker, Amy B. 2013. "Star Power? Advocacy, Receptivity, and Viewpoints on Celebrity Involvement in Issue Politics." *Atlantic Journal of Communication* 21 (1): 1–16.

Berkovich, Izhak. 2018. "Effects of Principal-Teacher Gender Similarity on Teacher's Trust and Organizational Commitment." *Sex Roles* 78 (7): 561–572.

Bernhard, Rachel, Mirya Holman, Shauna Shames, and Dawn Langan Teele. 2019. "Beyond Ambition." *Politics, Groups, and Identities* 7 (4): 815–816.

Berry, Justin A., David Ebner, and Michelle Cornelius. 2019. "White Identity Politics: Linked Fate and Political Participation." *Politics, Groups, and Identities* 9 (3): 519–537.

Bettinger, Eric P., and Bridget Terry Long. 2005. "Do Faculty Serve as Role Models? The Impact of Instructor Gender on Female Students." *American Economic Review* 95 (2): 152–157.

Betz, Diana E., and Denise Sekaquaptewa. 2012. "My Fair Physicist? Feminine Math and Science Role Models Demotivate Young Girls." *Social Psychological and Personality Science* 3 (6): 738–746.

Bhavnani, Rikhil R. 2009. "Do Electoral Quotas Work after They Are Withdrawn? Evidence from a Natural Experiment in India." *American Political Science Review* 103 (1): 23–35.

Biccum, April. 2011. "Marketing Development: Celebrity Politics and the 'New' Development Advocacy." *Third World Quarterly* 32 (7): 1331–1346.

Bloom, Allan. 1987. *The Closing of the American Mind: How Higher Education Has Failed Democracy and Impoverished the Souls of Today's Students.* New York: Simon & Schuster.

Bos, Angie, Jill Greenlee, Zoe Oxley, Mirya Holman, and J. Celeste Lay. 2021. "This One's for the Boys: How Gendered Political Socialization Limits Girls' Political Ambition and Interest." *American Political Science Review* 116 (2): 484–501.

Brady, Henry E., Sidney Verba, and Kay Lehman Schlozman. 1995. "Beyond SES: A Resource Model of Political Participation." *American Political Science Review* 89 (2): 271–294.

Bricheno, Patricia, and Mary Thornton. 2007. "Role Model, Hero or Champion? Children's Views Concerning Role Models." *Educational Research* 49 (4): 383–396.

Brockington, David, and Jeffrey Karp. 2002. "Social Desirability and Response Validity: A Comparative Analysis of Over-Reporting Turnout in Five Countries." Paper presented at the Annual Meeting of the American Political Science Association, Boston, MA.

Bromnick, Rachel D., and Brian L. Swallow. 1999. "I Like Being Who I Am: A Study of Young People's Ideals." *Educational Studies* 25 (2): 117–128.

Broockman, David E. 2014. "Do Female Politicians Empower Women to Vote or Run for Office? A Regression Discontinuity Approach." *Electoral Studies* 34:190–204.

Brooks, Deborah Jordan. 2006. "The Resilient Voter: Moving toward Closure in the Debate over Negative Campaigning and Turnout." *Journal of Politics* 68 (3): 684–696.

Buckley, William F. 1951. *God and Man at Yale: The Superstitions of "Academic Freedom."* Chicago: Regnery Publishing.

Budabin, Alexandra Cosima. 2020. "Caffeinated Solutions as Neoliberal Politics: How Celebrities Create and Promote Partnerships for Peace and Development." *Perspectives on Politics* 18 (1): 60–75.

Bush, George W. 2018. "Video and Full Transcript of George W. Bush's Eulogy for His Father." *New York Times*, December 5, 2018. Available at https://www.nytimes.com/2018/12/05/us/politics/george-w-bush-eulogy.html.

Campbell, David E. 2010. *Why We Vote.* Princeton, NJ: Princeton University Press.

Campbell, David E., and Christina Wolbrecht. 2006. "See Jane Run: Women Politicians as Role Models for Adolescents." *Journal of Politics* 68 (2): 233–247.

———. 2020. "The Resistance as Role Model: Disillusionment and Protest among American Adolescents after 2016." *Political Behavior* 42 (4): 1143–1168.

Carnes, Nicholas. 2012. "Does the Numerical Underrepresentation of the Working Class in Congress Matter?" *Legislative Studies Quarterly* 37 (1): 5–34.

Carnevale, Anthony P., Nicole Smith, and Michelle Melton. 2011. *STEM: Science Technology Engineering Mathematics.* Georgetown University Center on Education and the Workforce. Available at https://eric.ed.gov/?id=ED525307.

Carnevale, Anthony P., Nicole Smith, and Jeff Strohl. 2010. *Help Wanted: Projections of Job and Education Requirements through 2018.* Lumina Foundation. Available at https://eric.ed.gov/?id=ED524310.

Cheryan, Sapna, Benjamin J. Drury, and Marissa Vichayapai. 2013. "Enduring Influence of Stereotypical Computer Science Role Models on Women's Academic Aspirations." *Psychology of Women Quarterly* 37 (1): 72–79.

Cheryan, Sapna, John Oliver Siy, Marissa Vichayapai, Benjamin J. Drury, and Saenam Kim. 2011. "Do Female and Male Role Models Who Embody STEM Stereotypes Hinder Women's Anticipated Success in STEM?" *Social Psychological and Personality Science* 2 (6): 656–664.

Child, Irvin L. 1954. "Socialization." In *Special Fields and Applications*, 655–692. Vol. 2 of *Handbook of Social Psychology*, edited by Gardner Lindzey. Reading, MA: Addison-Wesley.

Childs, Sarah, and Melanie Hughes. 2018. "'Which Men?' How an Intersectional Perspective on Men and Masculinities Helps Explain Women's Political Under-Representation." *Politics and Gender* 14 (2): 282–287.

Choi, Chong Ju, and Ron Berger. 2010. "Ethics of Celebrities and Their Increasing Influence in 21st Century Society." *Journal of Business Ethics* 91:313–318.

Cicognani, Elvira, Bruna Zani, Bernard Fournier, Claire Gavray, and Michel Born. 2012. "Gender Differences in Youths' Political Engagement and Participation: The Role of Parents and of Adolescents' Social and Civic Participation." *Journal of Adolescence* 35 (3): 561–576.

Clayton, Dewey M., Sharon E. Moore, and Sharon D. Jones-Eversley. 2019. "The Impact of Donald Trump's Presidency on the Well-Being of African Americans." *Journal of Black Studies* 50 (8): 707–730.

Click, Melissa A., Hyunji Lee, and Holly Willson Holladay. 2017. "'You're Born to Be Brave': Lady Gaga's Use of Social Media to Inspire Fans' Political Awareness." *International Journal of Cultural Studies* 20 (6): 603–619.

Collins, Rebecca L. 1996. "For Better or Worse: The Impact of Upward Social Comparison on Self-Evaluations." *Psychological Bulletin* 119 (1): 51–69.

Corbett, Michael. 1991. *American Public Opinion*. White Plains, NY: Longman.

Coto, Jennifer, Elizabeth R. Pulgaron, Paulo A. Graziano, Daniel M. Bagner, Manuela Villa, Jamil A. Malik, and Alan M. Delamater. 2019. "Parents as Role Models: Associations between Parent and Young Children's Weight, Dietary Intake, and Physical Activity in a Minority Sample." *Maternal and Child Health Journal* 23 (7): 943–950.

Crowder-Meyer, Melody. 2020. "Baker, Bus Driver, Babysitter, Candidate? Revealing the Gendered Development of Political Ambition among Ordinary Americans." *Political Behavior* 42 (2): 359–384.

Czudnowski, Moshe. 1975. "Political Recruitment." In *Handbook of Political Science*, edited by Fred Greenstein and Nelson Polsby, 2:155–242. Reading, MA: Addison-Wesley.

Dabruzzi, Anthony, and Taurean Small. 2022. "'You Can't Have a Better Role Model than Gwen Moore': Mother-Son Duo Makes Wisconsin, U.S. Lawmaking a Family Affair." *Spectrum News 1*, February 25, 2022. Available at https://spectrumnews1.com/wi/madison/politics/2022/02/25/the-moores-makes-wisconsin--u-s--lawmaking-a-family-affair.

Dasgupta, Nilanjana. 2011. "Ingroup Experts and Peers as Social Vaccines Who Inoculate the Self-Concept: The Stereotype Inoculation Model." *Psychological Inquiry* 22 (4): 231–246.

Davies, James C. 1965. "The Family's Role in Political Socialization." *Annals of the American Academy of Political and Social Science* 361 (1): 10–19.

Deckman, Melissa. 2007. "Gender Differences in the Decision to Run for School Board." *American Politics Research* 35 (4): 541–563.

Deckman, Melissa, Jared McDonald, Stella Rouse, and Mileah Kromer. 2020. "Gen Z, Gender, and COVID-19." *Politics and Gender* 16 (4): 1019–1027.

Dee, Thomas S. 2004. "Teachers, Race, and Student Achievement in a Randomized Experiment." *Review of Economics and Statistics* 86 (1): 195–210.

Deininger, Klaus, and Yanyan Liu. 2013. "Economic and Social Impacts of an Innovative Self-Help Group Model in India." *World Development* 43:149–163.

Diekman, Amanda B., Emily K. Clark, Amanda M. Johnston, Elizabeth R. Brown, and Mia Steinberg. 2011. "Malleability in Communal Goals and Beliefs Influences Attraction to STEM Careers: Evidence for a Goal Congruity Perspective." *Journal of Personality and Social Psychology* 101 (5): 902–918.

Djupe, Paul A., and J. Tobin Grant. 2001. "Religious Institutions and Political Participation in America." *Journal for the Scientific Study of Religion* 40 (2): 303–314.

Dotti Sani, Giulia M., and Mario Quaranta. 2015. "Chips Off the Old Blocks? The Political Participation Patterns of Parents and Children in Italy." *Social Science Research* 50:264–276.

Driessens, Olivier. 2013. "The Celebritization of Society and Culture: Understanding the Structural Dynamics of Celebrity Culture." *International Journal of Cultural Studies* 16 (6): 641–657.

Dunifon, Rachel. 2013. "The Influence of Grandparents on the Lives of Children and Adolescents." *Child Development Perspectives* 7 (1): 55–60.

Eagly, Alice H. 2013. *Sex Differences in Social Behavior: A Social-Role Interpretation.* New York: Psychology Press.

Elliott, Rogers, A. Christopher Strenta, Russell Adair, Michael Matier, and Jannah Scott. 1996. "The Role of Ethnicity in Choosing and Leaving Science in Highly Selective Institutions." *Research in Higher Education* 37 (6): 681–709.

Farris, Emily M., and Mirya R. Holman. 2014. "Social Capital and Solving the Puzzle of Black Women's Political Participation." *Politics, Groups, and Identities* 2 (3): 331–349.

———. 2017. "All Politics Is Local? County Sheriffs and Localized Policies of Immigration Enforcement." *Political Research Quarterly* 70 (1): 142–154.

Fitzduff, Mari, ed. 2017. *Why Irrational Politics Appeals: Understanding the Allure of Trump.* Santa Barbara, CA: ABC-CLIO.

Foos, Florian, and Fabrizio Gilardi. 2020. "Does Exposure to Gender Role Models Increase Women's Political Ambition? A Field Experiment with Politicians." *Journal of Experimental Political Science* 7 (3): 157–166.

Friedersdorf, Conor. 2012. "Admit It, American Colleges Do Indoctrinate Students." *The Atlantic*, February 27, 2012. Available at https://www.theatlantic.com/politics/archive/2012/02/admit-it-american-colleges-do-indoctrinate-students/253607.

Frizzell, Craig. 2011. "Public Opinion and Foreign Policy: The Effects of Celebrity Endorsements." *The Social Science Journal* 48 (2): 314–323.

Fuesting, Melissa A., and Amanda B. Diekman. 2017. "Not by Success Alone: Role Models Provide Pathways to Communal Opportunities in STEM." *Personality and Social Psychology Bulletin* 43 (2): 163–176.

Gallup. n.d. "Party Affiliation." Available at https://news.gallup.com/poll/15370/party-affiliation.aspx. Accessed June 21, 2023.

Galston, William A. 2001. "Political Knowledge, Political Engagement, and Civic Education." *Annual Review of Political Science* 4 (1): 217–234.

Giani, Marco, and Pierre-Guillaume Méon. 2021. "Global Racist Contagion Following Donald Trump's Election." *British Journal of Political Science* 51 (3): 1332–1339.

Gibson, Donald E. 2004. "Role Models in Career Development: New Directions for Theory and Research." *Journal of Vocational Behavior* 65 (1): 134–156.

Gidengil, Elisabeth, Hannu Lahtinen, Hanna Wass, and Jani Erola. 2020. "From Generation to Generation: The Role of Grandparents in the Intergenerational Transmission of (Non-) Voting." *Political Research Quarterly* 74 (4): 1137–1151.

Gidengil, Elisabeth, Brenda O'Neill, and Lisa Young. 2010. "Her Mother's Daughter? The Influence of Childhood Socialization on Women's Political Engagement." *Journal of Women, Politics & Policy* 31 (4): 334–355.

Gidengil, Elisabeth, Hanna Wass, and Maria Valaste. 2016. "Political Socialization and Voting: The Parent-Child Link in Turnout." *Political Research Quarterly* 69 (2): 373–383.

Giersch, Jason. 2020. "Professors' Politics and Their Appeal as Instructors." *PS: Political Science and Politics* 53 (2): 281–285.

Giger, Nathalie, Jan Rosset, and Julian Bernauer. 2012. "The Poor Political Representation of the Poor in a Comparative Perspective." *Representation* 48 (1): 47–61.

Gilardi, Fabrizio. 2015. "The Temporary Importance of Role Models for Women's Political Representation." *American Journal of Political Science* 59 (4): 957–970.

Ginsburg, Ruth Bader. 2016. *In My Own Words*. New York: Simon & Schuster.

Giuliano, Paola, and Romain Wacziarg. 2020. "Who Voted for Trump? Populism and Social Capital." Working paper 27651, National Bureau of Economic Research.

Glick, Peter, and Susan T. Fiske. 1996. "The Ambivalent Sexism Inventory: Differentiating Hostile and Benevolent Sexism." *Journal of Personality and Social Psychology* 70 (3): 491–512.

Glick, Peter, Maria Lameiras, and Yolanda Rodriguez Castro. 2002. "Education and Catholic Religiosity as Predictors of Hostile and Benevolent Sexism toward Women and Men." *Sex Roles* 47 (9–10): 433–441.

Gniewosz, Burkhard, Peter Noack, and Monika Buhl. 2009. "Political Alienation in Adolescence: Associations with Parental Role Models, Parenting Styles, and Classroom Climate." *International Journal of Behavioral Development* 33 (4): 337–346.

Gordon, Hallie. 2022. "'Why Not Me?': The Boot Camp Giving Indigenous Women the Tools to Run for Office." *The Guardian*, April 17, 2022. Available at https://www.theguardian.com/us-news/2022/apr/17/indigenous-women-congress-native-action-network.

Graham, Bryan. 2016. "'Don't Boo, Vote!': Philly's History of Booing Makes Obama's Plea a Hard Sell." *The Guardian*, July 28, 2016. Available at https://www.theguardian.com/us-news/2016/jul/28/booing-philidelphia-losing-democratic-convention-sport.

Green, Jon, and Sean McElwee. 2019. "The Differential Effects of Economic Conditions and Racial Attitudes in the Election of Donald Trump." *Perspectives on Politics* 17 (2): 358–379.

Greenstein, Fred I. 1970. *Children and Politics*. New Haven, CT: Yale University Press.

Gross, Neil, and Solon Simmons, eds. 2014. *Professors and Their Politics*. Baltimore, MD: Johns Hopkins University Press.

Gunter, Barrie. 2014. *Celebrity Capital: Assessing the Value of Fame.* New York: Bloomsbury Publishing.

Halliday, Aria S., and Nadia E. Brown. 2018. "The Power of Black Girl Magic Anthems: Nicki Minaj, Beyoncé, and 'Feeling Myself' as Political Empowerment." *Souls* 20 (2): 222–238.

Hassan, Steven. 2020. *The Cult of trump: A Leading Cult Expert Explains How the President Uses Mind Control.* New York: Free Press.

Hayes, Michelle. 2022. "Social Media and Inspiring Physical Activity during COVID-19 and Beyond." *Managing Sport and Leisure* 27 (1–2): 8–15.

Hays, R. Allen, and Alexandra M. Kogl. 2007. "Neighborhood Attachment, Social Capital Building, and Political Participation: A Case Study of Low- and Moderate-Income Residents of Waterloo, Iowa." *Journal of Urban Affairs* 29 (2): 181–205.

Hernandez, Arthur E. 1995. "Do Role Models Influence Self Efficacy and Aspirations in Mexican American At-Risk Females?" *Hispanic Journal of Behavioral Sciences* 17 (2): 256–263.

Higgins, E. Tory. 1987. "Self-Discrepancy: A Theory Relating Self and Affect." *Psychological Review* 94 (3): 319–340.

Higgins, Monica C., and Kathy E. Kram. 2001. "Reconceptualizing Mentoring at Work: A Developmental Network Perspective." *Academy of Management Review* 26 (2): 264–288.

Higgs, Amy Lyons, and Victoria M. McMillan. 2006. "Teaching through Modeling: Four Schools' Experiences in Sustainability Education." *Journal of Environmental Education* 38 (1): 39–53.

Holbrook, Allyson L., and Jon A. Krosnick. 2010. "Social Desirability Bias in Voter Turnout Reports: Tests Using the Item Count Technique." *Public Opinion Quarterly* 74 (1): 37–67.

Holden, John. P., and Eric Lander. 2012. "Engage to Excel: Producing One Million Additional College Graduates with Degrees in Science, Technology, Engineering, and Mathematics." In *Report to the President*, edited by President's Council of Advisors on Science and Technology, vi. Washington, DC: Executive Office of the President.

Holman, Mirya R. 2014. *Women in Politics in the American City.* Philadelphia: Temple University Press.

Holman, Mirya R., and Monica C. Schneider. 2018. "Gender, Race, and Political Ambition: How Intersectionality and Frames Influence Interest in Political Office." *Politics, Groups, and Identities* 6 (2): 264–280.

Holmes, Julia G. 1993. "Teachers, Parents, and Children as Writing Role Models." *Dimensions of Early Childhood* 21 (3): 12–14.

Homolar, Alexandra, and Ronny Scholz. 2019. "The Power of Trump-Speak: Populist Crisis Narratives and Ontological Security." *Cambridge Review of International Affairs* 32 (3): 344–364.

Hooghe, Marc, and Ruth Dassonneville. 2018. "Explaining the Trump Vote: The Effect of Racist Resentment and Anti-Immigrant Sentiments." *PS: Political Science & Politics* 51 (3): 528–534.

Horowitz, David. 2010. *Reforming our Universities: The Campaign for an Academic Bill of Rights.* Chicago: Regnery Publishing.

Hoyt, Crystal L., Jeni L. Burnette, and Audrey N. Innella. 2012. "I Can Do That: The Impact of Implicit Theories on Leadership Role Model Effectiveness." *Personality and Social Psychology Bulletin* 38 (2): 257–268.

Hoyt, Crystal L., and Stefanie Simon. 2011. "Female Leaders: Injurious or Inspiring Role Models for Women?" *Psychology of Women Quarterly* 35 (1): 143–157.

Irvine, Jacqueline Jordan. 1989. "Beyond Role Models: An Examination of Cultural Influences on the Pedagogical Perspectives of Black Teachers." *Peabody Journal of Education* 66 (4): 51–63.

Jackson, David J. 2008. "Selling Politics: The Impact of Celebrities' Political Beliefs on Young Americans." *Journal of Political Marketing* 6 (4): 67–83.

Jang, S. Mo, and Hoon Lee. 2014. "When Pop Music Meets a Political Issue: Examining How 'Born This Way' Influences Attitudes toward Gays and Gay Rights Policies." *Journal of Broadcasting & Electronic Media* 58 (1): 114–130.

Jennings, M. Kent. 2007. "Political Socialization." In *The Oxford Handbook of Political Behavior*, edited by Russel Dalton and Hans Dieter Klingemann. New York: Oxford University Press.

Jennings, M. Kent, and Laura Stoker. 2004. "Social Trust and Civic Engagement across Time and Generations." *Acta Politica* 39 (4): 342–379.

Jones, Martha S. 2020. "Mary McLeod Bethune Was at the Vanguard of More than 50 Years of Black Progress." *Smithsonian Magazine*, July 2020. Available at https://www.smithsonianmag.com/history/mary-mcleod-bethune-vanguard-more-than-50-years-black-progress-180975202/.

Kalmoe, Nathan P., and Lilliana Mason. 2022. *Radical American Partisanship: Mapping Violent Hostility, Its Causes, and What It Means for Democracy.* Chicago: University of Chicago Press.

Karp, Jeffrey A., and Susan A. Banducci. 2008. "When Politics Is Not Just a Man's Game: Women's Representation and Political Engagement." *Electoral Studies* 27 (1): 105–115.

Katz, Richard. 2001. "The Problem of Candidate Selection and Models of Party Democracy." *Party Politics* 7:277–296.

Kelly-Woessner, April, and Matthew Woessner. 2008. "Conflict in the Classroom: Considering the Effects of Partisan Difference on Political Education." *Journal of Political Science Education* 4 (3): 265–285.

Klar, Samara, and Yanna Krupnikov. 2016. *Independent Politics.* Cambridge: Cambridge University Press.

Krueger, Norris F., Jr., and Deborah V. Brazeal. 1994. "Entrepreneurial Potential and Potential Entrepreneurs." *Entrepreneurship Theory and Practice* 18 (3): 91–104.

Ladam, Christina, Jeffrey J. Harden, and Jason H. Windett. 2018. "Prominent Role Models: High-Profile Female Politicians and the Emergence of Women as Candidates for Public Office." *American Journal of Political Science* 62 (2): 369–381.

Langton, Kenneth P., and M. Kent Jennings. 1968. "Political Socialization and the High School Civics Curriculum in the United States." *American Political Science Review* 62 (3): 852–867.

Lawless, Jennifer L., and Richard L. Fox. 2005. *It Takes a Candidate: Why Women Don't Run for Office.* Cambridge: Cambridge University Press.

———. 2010. *It Still Takes a Candidate: Why Women Don't Run for Office.* Cambridge: Cambridge University Press.

———. 2015. *Running from Office: Why Young Americans Are Turned Off to Politics.* New York: Oxford University Press.

Lee, Richard M., and Steven B. Robbins. 1995. "Measuring Belongingness: The Social Connectedness and the Social Assurance Scales." *Journal of Counseling Psychology* 42 (2): 232–241.

Leighley, Jan E., and Jonathan Nagler. 2013. *Who Votes Now?: Demographics, Issues, Inequality, and Turnout in the United States.* Princeton, NJ: Princeton University Press.

Lockwood, Penelope. 2006. "'Someone Like Me Can Be Successful': Do College Students Need Same-Gender Role Models?" *Psychology of Women Quarterly* 30 (1): 36–46.

Lockwood, Penelope, Christian H. Jordan, and Ziva Kunda. 2002. "Motivation by Positive or Negative Role Models: Regulatory Focus Determines Who Will Best Inspire Us." *Journal of Personality and Social Psychology* 83 (4): 854–864.

Lockwood, Penelope, and Ziva Kunda. 1997. "Superstars and Me: Predicting the Impact of Role Models on the Self." *Journal of Personality and Social Psychology* 73 (1): 91–103.

———. 1999. "Increasing the Salience of One's Best Selves Can Undermine Inspiration by Outstanding Role Models." *Journal of Personality and Social Psychology* 76 (2): 214–228.

———. 2000. "Outstanding Role Models: Do They Inspire or Demoralize Us?" In *Psychological Perspectives on Self and Identity*, edited by Abraham Tesser, Richard B. Felson, and Jerry M. Suls, 147–171. American Psychological Association. Available at https://doi.org/10.1037/10357-006.

Longo, Nicholas V., and Ross P. Meyer. 2006. "College Students and Politics: A Literature Review. CIRCLE Working Paper 46." *Center for Information and Research on Civic Learning and Engagement (CIRCLE), University of Maryland.*

Lumpkin, Angela. 2008. "Teachers as Role Models Teaching Character and Moral Virtues." *Journal of Physical Education, Recreation & Dance* 79 (2): 45–50.

Lutz, George. 2003. "Participation, Cognitive Involvement, and Democracy: When Do Low Turnout and Low Cognitive Involvement Make a Difference, and Why?" Paper presented at the European Consortium for Political Research Joint Sessions of Workshops, Edinburgh, UK.

Lynch, Robert, Emily Lynch, Michael Briga, Samuli Helle, Simon Chapman, and Nicolas Lynch. 2019. "Support for Populist Candidates in the 2016 Presidential Elections Predicted by Declining Social Capital and an Increase in Suicides." PsyArXiv preprint, submitted September 6, 2019. Available at https://doi.org/10.31234/osf.io/edn69.

Lyons, William, and John M. Scheb. 1999. "Early Voting and the Timing of the Vote: Unanticipated Consequences of Electoral Reform." *State and Local Government Review* 31:147–152.

Maestas, Cherie, Grant W. Neeley, and Lilliard E. Richardson Jr. 2003. "The State of Surveying Legislators: Dilemmas and Suggestions." *State Politics and Policy Quarterly* 3 (1): 90–108.

Majic, Samantha, Daniel O'Neill, and Michael Bernhard. 2020. "Celebrity and Politics." *Perspectives on Politics* 18 (1): 1–8.

Malhotra, Neil, and Connor Raso. 2007. "Racial Representation and U.S. Senate Apportionment." *Social Science Quarterly* 88 (4): 1038–1048.

Mann, Christopher B., Kevin Arceneaux, and David W. Nickerson. 2020. "Do Negatively Framed Messages Motivate Political Participation? Evidence from Four Field Experiments." *American Politics Research* 48 (1): 3–21.

Mansbridge, Jane. 1999. "Should Blacks Represent Blacks and Women Represent Women? A Contingent 'Yes.'" *Journal of Politics* 61:628–657.

Mariani, Mack D., and Gordon J. Hewitt. 2008. "Indoctrination U.? Faculty Ideology and Changes in Student Political Orientation." *PS: Political Science and Politics* 41 (4): 773–783.

Mariani, Mack., Bryan W. Marshall, and A. Lanethea Mathews-Schultz. 2015. "See Hillary Clinton, Nancy Pelosi, and Sarah Palin Run? Party, Ideology, and the Influence of Female Role Models on Young Women." *Political Research Quarterly* 68 (4): 716–731.

Marshall, Gordon and Scott, John, eds. 1998. "Political Socialization." In *A Dictionary of Sociology*, 549. Oxford: Oxford University Press.

Marx, David M., and Phillip Atiba Goff. 2005. "Clearing the Air: The Effect of Experimenter Race on Target's Test Performance and Subjective Experience." *British Journal of Social Psychology* 44 (4): 645–657.

Marx, David M., and Sei Jin Ko. 2012. "Superstars 'Like' Me: The Effect of Role Model Similarity on Performance under Threat." *European Journal of Social Psychology* 42 (7): 807–812.

Marx, David M., Allyce H. Monroe, Chris E. Cole, and Patricia N. Gilbert. 2013. "No Doubt About It: When Doubtful Role Models Undermine Men's and Women's Math Performance under Threat." *Journal of Social Psychology* 153 (5): 542–559.

Marx, David M., and Jasmin S. Roman. 2002. "Female Role Models: Protecting Women's Math Test Performance." *Personality and Social Psychology Bulletin* 28 (9): 1183–1193.

Mason, Lilliana. 2018. *Uncivil Agreement: How Politics Became Our Identity*. Chicago: University of Chicago Press.

Matland, Richard. 2005. "Enhancing Women's Political Participation: Legislative Recruitment and Electoral Systems." In *Women in Parliament: Beyond Numbers*, edited by Azza Karam and Julie Ballington, 93–111. Stockholm: IDEA Publishing.

McIntyre, Rusty B., René M. Paulson, and Charles G. Lord. 2003. "Alleviating Women's Mathematics Stereotype Threat through Salience of Group Achievements." *Journal of Experimental Social Psychology* 39 (1): 83–90.

Merelman, Richard M. 1986. "Domination, Self-Justification, and Self-Doubt: Some Social-Psychological Considerations." *Journal of Politics* 48 (2): 276–300.

Morgan, Stephen L., and Jiwon Lee. 2018. "Trump Voters and the White Working Class." *Sociological Science* 5:234–245.

Morgenroth, Thekla, Michelle K. Ryan, and Kim Peters. 2015. "The Motivational Theory of Role Modeling: How Role Models Influence Role Aspirants' Goals." *Review of General Psychology* 19 (4): 465–483.

Motel, Seth. 2014. "Who Runs for Office? A Profile of the 2%." Pew Research Center. September 3, 2014. Available at https://www.pewresearch.org/fact-tank/2014/09/03/who-runs-for-office-a-profile-of-the-2/.

Nauta, Margaret M., and Michelle L. Kokaly. 2001. "Assessing Role Model Influences on Students' Academic and Vocational Decisions." *Journal of Career Assessment* 9 (1): 81–99.

Naylor, Brian. 2021. "Read Trump's Jan. 6 Speech, a Key Part of Impeachment Trial." *NPR*, February 10, 2021. Available at https://www.npr.org/2021/02/10/966396848/read-trumps-jan-6-speech-a-key-part-of-impeachment-trial.

Neumark, David, and Rosella Gardecki. 1996. "Women Helping Women? Role-Model and Mentoring Effects on Female Ph.D. Students in Economics" *National Bureau of Economic Research Working Paper.*

Niemi, Richard G., Mary A. Hepburn, and Chris Chapman. 2000. "Community Service by High School Students: A Cure for Civic Ills?" *Political Behavior* 22 (1): 45–69.

Niemi, Richard G., and Jane Junn. 2005. *Civic Education: What Makes Students Learn.* New Haven, CT: Yale University Press.

Nisbett, Gwendelyn S., and Christina Childs DeWalt. 2016. "Exploring the Influence of Celebrities in Politics: A Focus Group Study of Young Voters." *Atlantic Journal of Communication* 24 (3): 144–156.

Oswald, Hans, and Christine Schmid. 1998. "Political Participation of Young People in East Germany." *German Politics* 7 (3): 147–164.

Pease, Andrew, and Paul R. Brewer. 2008. "The Oprah Factor: The Effects of a Celebrity Endorsement in a Presidential Primary Campaign." *The International Journal of Press/Politics* 13 (4): 386–400.

Pitkin, Hanna Fenichel. 1967. *The Concept of Representation.* Berkeley: University of California Press.

Putnam, Robert D. 2000. *Bowling Alone: The Collapse and Revival of American Community.* New York. Simon & Schuster.

Raaijmakers, Quinten A. W., Tom F.M.A. Verbogt, and Wilma A. M. Vollebergh. 1998. "Moral Reasoning and Political Beliefs of Dutch Adolescents and Young Adults." *Journal of Social Issues* 54 (3): 531–546.

Radu, Miruna, and Christophe Loué. 2008. "Motivational Impact of Role Models as Moderated by 'Ideal' vs. 'Ought Self-Guides' Identifications." *Journal of Enterprising Culture* 16 (4): 441–465.

Reichard, Gladys A. 1938. "Social Life." In *General Anthropology*, edited by Franz Boaz, 409–486. Boston: Health.

Rojek, Chris. 2015. *Presumed Intimacy: Parasocial Interaction in Media, Society and Celebrity Culture.* John Wiley & Sons.

Sanbonmatsu, Kira, and Kelly Dittmar. 2020. "Are You Ready to Run? Campaign Trainings and Women's Candidacies in New Jersey." In *Good Reasons to Run: Women and Political Candidacy*, edited by Shauna L. Shames, Rachel I. Bernhard, Mirya R. Holman, and Dawn Langan Teele, 193–202. Philadelphia: Temple University Press.

Sapiro, Virginia. 2004. "Not Your Parents' Political Socialization: Introduction for a New Generation." *Annual Review of Political Science* 7:1–23.

Schaffner, Brian F., Matthew MacWilliams, and Tatishe Nteta. 2018. "Understanding White Polarization in the 2016 Vote for President: The Sobering Role of Racism and Sexism." *Political Science Quarterly* 133 (1): 9–34.

Schneider, Monica C., and Angela L. Bos. 2014. "Measuring Stereotypes of Female Politicians." *Political Psychology* 35 (2): 245–266.

Schneider, Monica C., and Mirya R. Holman. 2020. "Can Role Models Help Increase Women's Desire to Run? Evidence from Political Psychology." In *Politicking While Female: The Political Lives of Women*, edited by Nichole Bauer. Baton Rouge: Louisiana State University Press.

Schneider, Monica C., Mirya R. Holman, Amanda B. Diekman, and Thomas McAndrew. 2016. "Power, Conflict, and Community: How Gendered Views of Political Power Influence Women's Political Ambition." *Political Psychology* 37 (4): 515–531.

Schneider, Monica C., and Jennie Sweet-Cushman. 2020. "Pieces of Women's Political Ambition Puzzle: Changing Perceptions of a Political Career with Campaign Training." In *Good Reasons to Run: Women and Political Candidacy*, edited by Shauna L. Shames, Rachel I. Bernhard, Mirya R. Holman, and Dawn Langan Teele, 203–214. Philadelphia: Temple University Press.

Schneider, Monica C., Jennie Sweet-Cushman, and Taylor Gordon. 2023. "Role Model Do No HARM: Modeling Achievable Success Inspires Social Belonging and Women's Candidate Emergence." *Journal of Women, Politics and Policy* 44 (1): 105–120.

Schuler, Paul. 2019. "Female Autocrats as Role Models? The Effect of Female Leaders on Political Knowledge and Engagement in Vietnam." *Journal of Politics* 81 (4): 1546–1550.

Schuman, Howard, Charlotte Steeh, Lawrence Bobo, and Maria Krysan. 1997. *Racial Attitudes in America: Trends and Interpretations*. Cambridge, MA: Harvard University Press.

Schwartz, David. 1969. "Toward a Theory of Political Recruitment." *Western Political Quarterly* 22:552–571.

Shames, Shauna Lani. 2017. "Intersectionality and Political Ambition." In *Oxford Research Encyclopedia of Politics*, edited by William R. Thompson. New York: Oxford University Press.

Shapiro, Ben. 2010. *Brainwashed: How Universities Indoctrinate America's Youth*. Nashville: Thomas Nelson.

Shaw, Rissa. 2021. "Central Texas Man Charged in U.S. Capitol Riot 'Relieved and Thankful' Following Federal Judges' Release." *KWTX*, February 22, 2021. Available at https://www.kwtx.com/2021/02/22/federal-judge-releases-central-texas-man-charged-in-us-capitol-riot/.

Shields, Jon A., and Joshua M. Dunn. 2016. "Do Universities Need Affirmative Action for Conservative Professors?" *Los Angeles Times*, March 18, 2016. Available at https://www.latimes.com/opinion/op-ed/la-oe-0320-shields-dunn-conservative-affirmative-action-20160320-story.html.

Shin, Jiyun Elizabeth L., Sheri R. Levy, and Bonita London. 2016. "Effects of Role Model Exposure on STEM and Non-STEM Student Engagement." *Journal of Applied Social Psychology* 46 (7): 410–427.

Silverman, D., N. Gartrell, M. Aronson, M. Steer, and S. Edbril. 1983. "In Search of the Biopsychosocial Perspective: An Experiment with Beginning Medical Students." *American Journal of Psychiatry* 140 (9): 1154–1159.

Singh, Val, Susan Vinnicombe, and Kim James. 2006. "Constructing a Professional Identity: How Young Female Managers Use Role Models." *Women in Management Review* 21 (1): 67–81.

Smith, David G., and Judith E. Rosenstein. 2017. "Gender and the Military Profession: Early Career Influences, Attitudes, and Intentions." *Armed Forces and Society* 43 (2): 260–279.

Smith, Elizabeth S. 1999. "The Effects of Investments in the Social Capital of Youth on Political and Civic Behavior in Young Adulthood: A Longitudinal Analysis." *Political Psychology* 20 (3): 553–580.

Smith, Ken G., and Michael A. Hitt, eds. 2005. *Great Minds in Management: The Process of Theory Development*. New York: Oxford University Press.

Sosik, John J., and Veronica M. Godshalk. 2000. "The Role of Gender in Mentoring: Implications for Diversified and Homogenous Mentoring Relationships." *Journal of Vocational Behavior* 57 (1): 102–122.

Stephens, Elizabeth H., and Joseph A. Dearani. 2021. "On Becoming a Master Surgeon: Role Models, Mentorship, Coaching, and Apprenticeship." *Annals of Thoracic Surgery* 111 (6): 1746–1753.

Stoker, Laura, and M. Kent Jennings. 1995. "Life-Cycle Transitions and Political Participation: The Case of Marriage." *American Political Science Review* 89 (2): 421–433.

Stolle, Dietlind, and Marc Hooghe. 2004. "The Roots of Social Capital: Attitudinal and Network Mechanisms in the Relation between Youth and Adult Indicators of Social Capital." *Acta Politica* 39 (4): 422–441.

Street, John. 2019. "What is Donald Trump? Forms of 'Celebrity' in Celebrity Politics." *Political Studies Review* 17 (1): 3–13.

Strenta, A. Christopher, Rogers Elliott, Russell Adair, Michael Matier, and Jannah Scott. 1994. "Choosing and Leaving Science in Highly Selective Institutions." *Research in Higher Education* 35 (5): 513–547.

Sweet-Cushman, Jennie. 2014. "Individual Differences in Psychological Evaluations of Electoral Risk: Furthering the Explanation of the Gender Gap in Candidate Emergence." Ph.D. diss., Wayne State University.

———. 2018a. "See It; Be It? The Use of Role Models in Campaign Trainings for Women." *Politics, Groups, and Identities* 7 (4): 853–863.

———. 2018b. "Where Does the Pipeline Get Leaky? The Progressive Ambition of School Board Members and Personal and Political Network Recruitment." *Politics, Groups, and Identities* 8 (4): 762–785.

———. 2021. "Legislative vs. Executive Political Offices: How Gender Stereotypes Can Disadvantage Women in Either Office." *Political Behavior* 44: 1–24.

Sydell, Laura. 2017. "On Both the Left and Right, Trump Is Driving New Political Engagement." *NPR Morning Edition*, March 3, 2017.

Tesser, Abraham. 1991. "Emotion in Social Comparison and Reflection Processes." In *Social Comparison: Contemporary Theory and Research*, edited by J. Suls and T. A. Wills, 115–145. Mahwah, NJ: Lawrence Erlbaum Associates.

Tesser, Abraham, and Jennifer Campbell. 1983. "Self-Definition and Self-Evaluation Maintenance." In *Social Psychological Perspectives on the Self*, edited by Jerry Suls and Anthony Greenwald, 2:1–31. United Kingdom: Lawrence Erlbaum Associates.

Tonidandel, Scott, Derek R. Avery, and McKensy G. Phillips. 2007. "Maximizing Returns on Mentoring: Factors Affecting Subsequent Protégé Performance." *Journal of Organizational Behavior: The International Journal of Industrial, Occupational and Organizational Psychology and Behavior* 28 (1): 89–110.

Towler, Christopher C., Nyron N. Crawford, and Robert A. Bennett. 2020. "Shut Up and Play: Black Athletes, Protest Politics, and Black Political Action." *Perspectives on Politics* 18 (1): 111–127.

Turban, Daniel B., Thomas W. Dougherty, and Felissa K. Lee. 2002. "Gender, Race, and Perceived Similarity Effects in Developmental Relationships: The Moderating Role of Relationship Duration." *Journal of Vocational Behavior* 61 (2): 240–262.

U.S. Congress. 2021. *Impeaching Donald John Trump, President of the United States, for High Crimes and Misdemeanors.* H. R. 24, 117th Cong., 1st Sess., introduced January 11, 2021. Available at https://www.congress.gov/117/bills/hres24/BILLS -117hres24ih.pdf.

Verba, Sidney, and Norman H. Nie. 1972. *Participation in America: Social Equality and Political Democracy.* New York: Harper Collins.

Verba, Sidney, Kay Lehman Schlozman, and Henry E. Brady. 1995. *Voice and Equality: Civic Voluntarism in American Politics.* Cambridge, MA: Harvard University Press.

Verba, Sidney, Kay Lehman Schlozman, and Nancy Burns. 2005. "Family Ties: Understanding the Intergenerational Transmission of Political Participation." In *The Social Logic of Politics: Personal Networks as Contexts for Political Behavior*, edited by Alan Zuckerman, 95–114. Philadelphia: Temple University Press.

Vesey, Alyxandra. 2015. "Putting Her on the Shelf: Pop Star Fragrances and Post-Feminist Entrepreneurialism." *Feminist Media Studies* 15 (6): 992–1008.

Walsh, Katherine Cramer, M. Kent Jennings, and Laura Stoker. 2004. "The Effects of Social Class Identification on Participatory Orientations towards Government." *British Journal of Political Science* 34 (3): 469–495.

Walsh, Kenneth T. 2017. "The Missing Role Models: Public Officials Used to Be Worthy of Being Looked Up To—Not Anymore." *U.S. News & World Report*, December 1, 2017. Available at https://www.usnews.com/news/the-report/articles/2017-12 -01/there-are-no-role-models-left-in-politics.

Wauters, Bram, and Hilde Van Liefferinge. 2017. "Does Family Politicization Affect Party Membership Activity? A Study of Four Flemish Parties." *PCS–Politics, Culture and Socialization* 6 (1+2): 19–20.

Weller, Nicholas, and Jane Junn. 2018. "Racial Identity and Voting: Conceptualizing White Identity in Spatial Terms." *Perspectives on Politics* 16 (2): 436–448. Available at https://doi.org/10.1017/S1537592717004285.

Whitehead, Andrew L., Samuel L. Perry, and Joseph O. Baker. 2018. "Make America Christian Again: Christian Nationalism and Voting for Donald Trump in the 2016 Presidential Election." *Sociology of Religion* 79 (2): 147–171.

Wiese, Bettina S., and Alexandra M. Freund. 2011. "Parents as Role Models: Parental Behavior Affects Adolescents' Plans for Work Involvement." *International Journal of Behavioral Development* 35 (3): 218–224.

Wigfield, Allan, and Jacquelynne S. Eccles. 2000. "Expectancy–Value Theory of Achievement Motivation." *Contemporary Educational Psychology* 25 (1): 68–81.

Wolak, Jennifer. 2015. "Candidate Gender and the Political Engagement of Women and Men." *American Politics Research* 43 (5): 872–896.

Wolbrecht, Christina, and David E. Campbell. 2007. "Leading by Example: Female Members of Parliament as Political Role Models." *American Journal of Political Science* 51 (4): 921–939.

Wooldridge, Adrian. 2005. "The Brains Business: A Survey of Higher Education." *The Economist*, September 10, 2005. Available at https://www.economist.com/special -report/2018/08/14/the-brains-business.

YouGov. n.d. "The Most Famous Politicians." Available at https://today.yougov.com /ratings/politics/fame/politicians/all. Accessed May 10, 2022.

Index

Jennie Sweet-Cushman is Associate Professor of Political Science at Chatham University.